HARBOUR
MANOEUVRES
STEP-BY-STEP

HARBOUR
MANOEUVRES
STEP-BY-STEP

LARS BOLLE & KLAUS ANDREWS

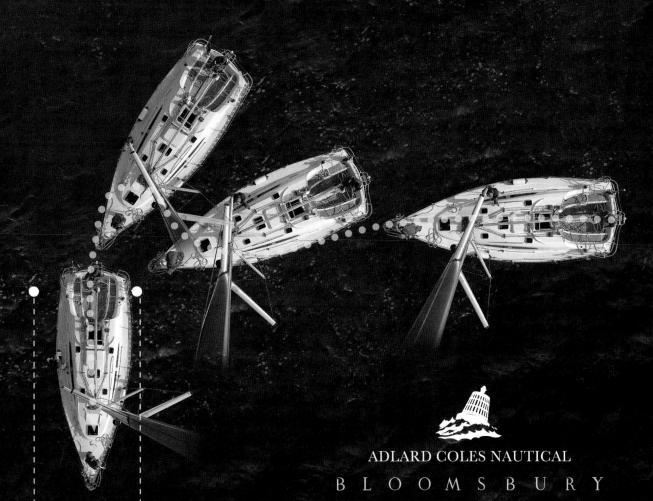

ADLARD COLES NAUTICAL

B L O O M S B U R Y
LONDON · NEW DELHI · NEW YORK · SYDNEY

Published by Adlard Coles Nautical
an imprint of Bloomsbury Publishing Plc
50 Bedford Square, London WC1B 3DP
www.adlardcoles.com

Copyright © 2011 by Delius, Klasing & Co. KG, Bielefeld

Published in 2011 by Delius Klasing Verlag, Bielefeld under the title *Hafenmonöver Schritt für Schritt*

Published in the UK in 2012 by Adlard Coles Nautical

ISBN 978-1-4081-5895-1

A CIP catalogue record for this book is available from the British Library.

This book is produced using paper that is made from wood grown in managed, sustainable forests. It is natural, renewable and recyclable. The logging and manufacturing processes conform to the environmental regulations of the country of origin.

Typeset in 9 pt Utopia Std by Margaret Brain
Printed and bound in Croatia by Zrinski

Note: while all reasonable care has been taken in the publication of this book, the publisher takes no responsibility for the use of the methods or products described in the book.

Contents

Practise, practise, practise . . .

Harbour manoeuvres can be tricky. There's not much space to manoeuvre, and with a big yacht and an unprepared crew the result can be chaos. But this can be avoided with forethought and training.

It's not sailing that demands the crew's greatest concentration – as surveys have shown, the fewest number of problems occur at sea. For those who responded, the most worrying time was berthing and sailing away, particularly in very windy conditions. And let's face it: whose heart doesn't beat faster the more densely packed the entrance to the harbour or the anchorage, whether it be the tenth or the hundredth approach. There's no shame either in being concerned when a yacht that was designed for demands at sea and not for the specialized conditions in harbour approaches a dock under quite a small motor.

To make matters worse, in the majority of cases experiences can't be transferred directly from one yacht to another. People say you never forget how to ride a bike or drive a car, but the same is only true for harbour manoeuvres to a much lesser degree. For every different design of yacht, be it a long or short keeler, a heavy steel displacement hull or a light displacement hull, there are just as many different types of behaviour while manoeuvring. Anyone who changes their yacht has to learn to manoeuvre all over again. Those who charter boats have it particularly hard in this respect. Even if they don't think about it and just assume it's really a lack of practice that's causing them to make mistakes, they've still got to live with the particular handicap of the ever-changing size and type of yacht.

Developments in boat-building don't help with behaviour in harbour, quite the opposite. Even though modern leisure craft with their short keels are easier to manoeuvre than their long-keeled predecessors and are much easier to steer backwards, other features can more than cancel out these advantages.

Let's compare older and newer yachts. If a manoeuvre goes wrong and you have to correct your position by muscle power, then quite often more strength is needed with the modern yacht, because yachts aren't bigger just in absolute terms. This size isn't just a matter of length. Looking at trends in production boats a further trend is clearly discernible: the more modern a yacht is, the bigger the surface she offers to the wind in proportion to her lateral surface, as can be seen in the diagram on p. 13. Or to put it more simply: there's more and more above the waterline, and less and less below it.

Every square metre counts. In a Force 6 wind one square metre more offers a significant resistance to the wind. To put it simply, you have to pull on the mooring rope with an additional twelve kilograms or so to stop the boat at the mooring (see table on p. 10). Anyone who's ever tried to pull a boat forwards or backwards along the dock by hand in a Force 6 wind will tell you what that means in practice. This often won't work without a winch or without using your own body weight. In this situation modern boats have more of an advantage because they have longer cabins and straighter sterns. Take the bow for example: older boats

Overcrowded harbours are the norm these days. You can't avoid having to manoeuvre in the narrowest of spaces.

1 m² approx.

No holding back

Pressure on the hull and the rigging increases by the square of the wind speed. The table shows the values over the Beaufort range. To illustrate it better the Newtons have been converted to kilograms. You have to set this weight against a surface standing vertical to the wind direction with the drag coefficient cw=1, so that it doesn't blow away. An approximately flat circular disk has a cw-value of 1. Depending on how much a part of the hull surface is curved concavely or convexly, and also depending on its outline, a higher or lower cw-value will result. For comparison purposes an average value of 1 is useful and has been used.

Wind pressure on a surface of one square metre with $c_w=1$

Wind strength on the Beaufort scale	Windspeed in m/s	Wind pressure in N/m²	Wind pressure in kg/m²
0	0.2	0.03	0.003
up to 1	1.5	1.4	0.1
up to 2	3.3	6.6	0.7
up to 3	5.4	17.6	1.8
up to 4	7.9	37.6	3.8
up to 5	10.7	68.9	7.0
up to 6	13.8	115	11.7
up to 7	17.1	176	17.9
up to 8	20.7	258	26.3
up to 9	24.7	367	37.4

almost always have a very raked stem, while nowadays stern shapes are closer and closer to the vertical. The triangle from the bow to the waterline which used to be open is now almost completely filled, giving an extra point of attack for the wind. The situation is the same for cabin structure. It's often actually no higher in absolute terms than before, but this height is drawn out further. If you imagine the side elevation of the hull framed by a rectangle, then the body and superstructure lines of older yachts only touch this frame now and then, whilst modern yachts fill it much more.

In addition the mast nowadays is located considerably further forward and is taller. Everyone can see that immediately in harbour, but what you can't see immediately is what this means. The projected surface of a 13-metre-long mast with a profile depth of 25 centimetres is something like an an entire Optimist sail! In addition there's the trend towards a furled headsail; hardly a single new cruising yacht leaves the boatyard without one. For, say, a 12 metre luff length a rolled up genoa with a diameter of just 10 centimetres gives a projected surface of 1.2 square metres, and well forward on the boat at that. For yachts with a boom length of 4.5 metres and a bag height of 40 centimetres there is an extra 1.8 square metres of windage. And on a modern yacht this is probably three metres or more above the surface of the water, since the large boom is fixed higher was normal, to make a roomy sprayhood possible.

All-in-all an average 10-metre cruising boat today offers more than 20 square metres of attack surface to the wind above the waterline, not counting the stays, shrouds, spreaders, bow or stern pulpits ... that's 10 to 15 per cent more than 20 years ago.

From the correct starting position, even a stern first manoeuvre can be managed (above left). If all else fails use muscle power, though a well-placed line would have been better (above right). Sometimes a collision is inevitable. Then it's better to risk a scratch to the boat than an injury to yourself.

ne out WHV 278

However, the key to the manoeuvring behaviour of modern yachts is found beneath the waterline. Modern designs have a pronounced U-shaped hull. This offers a larger beam in the forefoot area, and produces a particularly high dimensional stability which means you don't need so much ballast. This is necessary since modern boats aren't much lighter than their predecessors and in spite of more efficient methods of construction. In comparison to the waterline length, modern yachts are on a par with older ones in terms of unit kg per metre. But this is an unfair comparison because the laminate of modern yachts takes up a greater volume and modern hulls are essentially wider than before, particularly at the stern where there is a large surface area. In addition the hulls provide space for more interior fittings and equipment than before.

The U-shaped hull is the form with the smallest wetted surface and is the only possible one for a wide stern in which one or two double bunks must be accommodated. A moderate S-shaped or trapezium-shaped frame, as shown by the IOR yachts up to the end of the 1980s, would have a much greater wetted surface for the same width and thus too much resistance. Actually, designers have managed to make modern yachts sail faster than their predecessors despite having so much volume. This was achieved by more effective and narrower attachments, viewed from the side. The ballast is concentrated mostly in a bulb, the keel fin over it and the rudder blades have become shorter and shorter. Altogether the projecting lateral surface has decreased – the surface which inhibits sideways movement through the water.

Thus the projecting surface underwater continually decreases and, what's more, calculating a projecting surface for a U-shaped hull is very misleading, since the vertical and thus most effectively resistant part is extremely small. To put it simply: under water, modern boats are bowls that lie flat on the water (see also p.15). That also explains the observation from practice that, with the wind abeam, the bow turns more strongly than on older designs, although the waterline is longer. The additional surface through the straight stem doesn't offer enough resistance under water, as is the case with the trapezium or S-shaped frame. In modern design the first effective surface begins more or less with the keel fin in the middle of the hull!

All these factors taken together make it clear that boats nowadays are generally more susceptible to crosswinds than their predecessors. However, this is not a problem when the boat is moving at speed. In that case the keel-rudder arrangement produces enough directional stability to come cleanly through the harbour. In particular the centre of rotation is precisely defined through the clear division of the lateral plan, so a boat nowadays turns well on the corners and manoeuvres more agilely than an IOR-boat or a long-keeler. In addition motors are significantly more powerful than before, so a stronger propeller wash is produced.

So it's actually easier to reach a mooring. But having got there, there will be problems in a fresh breeze. When they're not under way large modern yachts are at the mercy of the wind. If the first approach isn't successful or has to be stopped the situation can get dangerous. A turning manoeuvre in a narrow marina lane may then no longer be possible, and the danger of sailing into an obstacle is correspondingly greater. And this isn't helped by modern wheel design where the turning capacity is limited mechanically to a maximum of 40 degrees. The old trick of turning the stern round with a free moving tiller is no longer possible.

And then there's something else to consider which has nothing to do with the lateral surface or the shape of the hull: boats have simply become larger. Although a yacht with a hull length of just over nine metres was once considered every sailing family's dream, today the entry model alone of many boatyards is 10 metres long. However, space in marinas has not kept pace with the size of boats. The lanes of mooring spaces have instead become even narrower. This increase in boat size is even clearer in the charter sector. At a rough estimate, charter boats are growing by about three feet of hull length every decade – but the size of the crew remains the same. The extra space is necessary for the increase in comfort that is demanded. However, harbours are not expanding, so space for manoeuvring is decreasing. At the same time the size of boats, and with it their slowness of movement, is greater

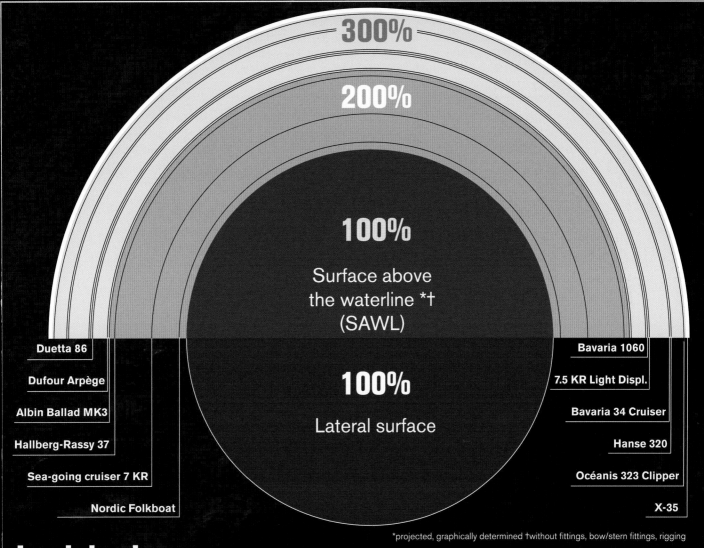

Left side labels (outer to inner): Duetta 86, Dufour Arpège, Albin Ballad MK3, Hallberg-Rassy 37, Sea-going cruiser 7 KR, Nordic Folkboat

Right side labels (inner to outer): Bavaria 1060, 7.5 KR Light Displ., Bavaria 34 Cruiser, Hanse 320, Océanis 323 Clipper, X-35

300%

200%

100%
Surface above
the waterline *†
(SAWL)

100%
Lateral surface

*projected, graphically determined †without fittings, bow/stern fittings, rigging

Lavish above the waterline

The diagram shows the ratio of lateral surface to surface above the waterline of some selected craft, and in the table (right) some additional types are listed. It's noticeable that the newer the boats are, the bigger the proportion of the hull surface is above water.

Moreover, the proportion is all the more marked the smaller the length of the hull. In other words: the smaller a boat is, the more it has to be exploited in all dimensions to follow the trend for more and more volume. But something else is also clear. Take, for example, the X-35: not only does the volume increase, but also the lateral surface is reduced because of the U-shaped hull and the narrow attachments.

TYPE	YEAR OF CONSTRUCTION	SAWL*	TYPE	YEAR OF CONSTRUCTION	SAWL*
7.5 KR Light Displ.	1960	237	Dufour Arpège	1970	204
Albin Ballad Mk3	1984	202	Elan 34	2006	253
Bavaria 1060	1985	230	Hallberg-Rassy 36	1990	200
Bavaria 31 Cruiser	2007	276	Hallberg-Rassy 37	2003	195
Bavaria 34 Cruiser	2007	270	Hanse 320	2007	271
Bavaria 35 Match	2004	245	Centreboards	1940	128
Bavaria 38 Cruiser	2007	264	Nordic Folkboat	1940	109
Bavaria 50 Cruiser	2005	234	Océanis 31	2008	252
Comfortina 32	1987	225	Océanis 323 Clipper	2003	298
Comfortina 35	1993	241	Sea-going cruiser 7 KR	1950	142
Dehler 34	2007	280	Sea cruiser 'Coronel II'	1930	107
Dehler 34/Optima 101	1980	205	Sun Odyssey 32i	2002	224
Dehler 44	2006	280	Sunbeam 44	1996	254
Delphia 33	2007	248	X-34	2007	229
Duetta 86	1980	228	X-35	2006	303
Dufour 325	2005	271	X-99	1985	251
Dufour 34 Performance	2003	305	*surface above waterline		

In the Mediterranean Sea, the main destination of charterers, an important aid to mooring is lacking: mooring posts. In the north a botched harbour manoeuvre can usually be sorted out because you can tie up at a mooring post and haul on a line in peace. Just about anything can be corrected by targeted use of a line, as will be explained in detail in the following chapters. This is not the case with berthing at moorings and anchoring. If you don't get the approach right, there's always a danger that you'll get caught in other chains or lines and only manage to get free with the help of other people.

Therefore nowadays it's just as important as it ever was to prepare carefully for berthing or sailing-away manoeuvres. Knowing the boat also comes into it. If it has a propshaft a strong inflow from the rudder blade can be counted on when making headway, but prop walk must be taken into account. By contrast, with a Saildrive the inflow is not so direct, indeed it hardly develops any prop walk. A long keeler may not steer well astern and will break out, so that time after time you have to react with forward thrusts on the motor. A short keeler by contrast normally runs astern very stably, but drifts away as soon as the boat loses speed.

The features described have brought us to the point where we need to go back a few decades – when yachts didn't have motors – and use handling lines. Used correctly, a handling line can defuse many a hair-raising manoeuvre. It's generally the case that a line between the boat and the shore is enough to bring the yacht safely to her mooring.

This book presents the various ways of approaching or leaving a mooring with or without the help of a line, be it alongside or across a pontoon or in a port facility with posts and jetties or landing stages. The individual manoeuvres will be presented step-by-step, the relevant rudder positions will be shown together with the strength and direction of the thrust of the engine. Manoeuvres that are particularly suitable for single-handed sailors are identified in the table of contents. Thus we're talking mostly about manoeuvres that can be accomplished stern first. They're just as effective for small crews, i.e. two-person crews, and suitable for crews with a number of inexperienced sailors where the helmsman mainly has to fend for himself.

To master these manoeuvres they have to be practised over and over again, there's no getting round that. This is even more true for another basic set of harbour manoeuvres: those carried out under sail. Of course, harbours these days are very narrow, yachts are very large, and motors very reliable. And yet of course it can happen, particularly when it's very windy and the sea's very high, that the sediment in the fuel tank is churned up and the fuel filter becomes blocked. Then there's nothing for it but to trust in your own abilities. Practice is of course even more important for sailing manoeuvres, where you need to calculate your speed and the remaining distance as well as the course. Because every boat reacts completely differently depending on her draught, the shape of the hull and keel as well as the sails, the skipper must develop a feeling for how much way the boat carries and how she reacts to the movement of the rudder under full sail or just under mainsail or headsail. So get a feeling for the boat as described in the appropriate chapter – and of course when using the engine as well.

In addition we'll talk about using the correct anchor. For one thing it's a permanent component of harbour manoeuvres in many Mediterranean marinas, and for another you'll need it when you seek protection from the open sea and anchor in a bay.

Further chapters deal with towing and man overboard manoeuvres and so round off this guidebook to manoeuvring.

Flat bowls

Modern cruisers and racing yachts display distinctly U-shaped sections. This offers a great deal of volume in the floor area and potentially better reaching characteristics – for racing yachts it makes earlier planing possible. But it's most inconvenient when you have to balance resistance with displacement. The more vertical a surface is to the water, the greater its resistance. It's not the keel itself that we're talking about here, but the shape of the main sections. The narrower these are at the waterline the deeper they must be to offer the same volume, to put it very simply. The deeper the hull is the closer it approaches the form of a plate. So, the smaller the curve and the bigger the plate, the better. The U-shaped frame of modern boats has the smallest vertical element of all, it's like a flat bowl on the water and presents the least obstacle for the current in a sideways direction. On the other hand the S-shaped frame of a long-keeler is almost a guarantee against uncontrolled sideways movement.

S-shaped section   **U-shaped section**

V-shaped section   **Trapezium-shaped section**

Radial section   **Double-angled section**

Don't be over sensitive with the throttle control. Large boats need many short bursts.

Sometimes you have to push off by hand, but you shouldn't use the guard rails.

A lee shore situation onto other boats or anchor chains is very unpleasant.

This mooring line has a loop, which the crew has pushed through the cleat and then around it. He can then proceed with the working end as described.

Tying up

How to deal with lines when berthing and sailing away

Belaying on a cleat

Round turn, figure of eight, locking turn: these three terms should be imprinted like a mantra on anyone who goes on board a boat. Then even an occasional sailor who finds himself in an awkward situation when manoeuvring in harbour can manage to tie up. You should know how to belay on a cleat since they're available on most boats and many landing stages. Cleats achieve their effect through friction. By tying a figure of eight you lengthen the section on which friction can work. In addition you can increase it with a sharp tug on the horns. This is how you do it: **1** Take the mooring line round the cleat so that it already has sufficient friction. The standing end must lead away from the cleat, otherwise the working end could jam. (As shown here the line is also under control if it needs to be paid out during any manoeuvres. Muscle power is then hardly needed.) **2** After the first round turn take the working end in a figure of eight round the horns as often as you need until there's no more tension on the working end **3** otherwise final locking turn could jam. At the end the locking turn should only serve to hold the figure of eight in place. **4** Throw the locking turn the correct way so that all the figures of eight lie parallel.

This is general procedure for throwing a line: the receiver will be pleased that a wet bundle doesn't catch him a wallop, almost knocking him over and instead one or two bights of rope reach him with one well-aimed throw. However, he's even more pleased to get a line handed to him. If that happens the tying up manoeuvre is quite perfect. Sometimes, however, you won't be able to avoid having to throw over a good distance, so always prepare a long manoeuvring line, ready to be thrown as needed.

This is how you do it: **1** Coil the line in bights in one hand. **2** Take two or three bights in the throwing hand, depending on the thickness of the line and the strength of the thrower. Let one bight drop so that it's ready to throw. **3** Throw the bights you've taken in your throwing hand to shore or to another boat, **4** and as you do so open the other hand (with the coiled bundle) in the direction of the throw **5** so that as much of the line as is needed can run out.

A running loop

A Belaying on shore is the same as on board: don't overdo it. Here too many round turns and figures-of-eight have been laid on the cleat.

B On the other hand, if you're tying up with a single loop a safer method is to pull it through the cleat and then lay it over the top.

A

B

You can tie up to a mooring post by simply passing a loop over it or tying the mooring line round it with a loop knot. However, if the mooring post doesn't have hooks or something similar the mooring line can slip downwards. Dirty harbour water is then the lesser of two evils: a loop sliding down over a densely overgrown mooring post can chafe and the mooring rope can be cut. On the other hand the variation shown with a running loop helps. It's also suitable when you're trying to berth and find that the loop is too small for the circumference of the mooring post or when there's a danger that that the loop will slip off the top of the mooring post when the water level rises. However this method has a serious drawback: yachts which arrive later can only lay their mooring lines over yours, which will obstruct it, so a running loop should only be used if you're tying up for a long time at your own berth or by arrangement with neighbouring boats at a guest mooring.

Pulling through a loop

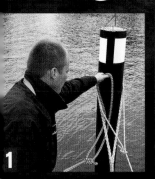

1

2

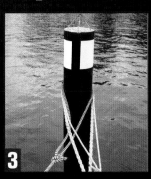

3

If a mooring post already has other lines on it, the loop of your own mooring line cannot simply be laid over them, since it will obstruct the other lines. If the boat next to you wants to sail away he'll have to untie the bowline on his own line or, if the loop is spliced, first remove your mooring line. So don't be surprised if in the morning your mooring line is hanging in the water or if your neighbour asks you to remove your mooring line because he wants to sail away. Therefore pass your own loop as shown **1** and **2** underneath and through the other one and **3** only then loop it over the mooring post. That way you'll allow

Extensions

A boathook is very useful as an extension of your arm when laying a loop over a mooring post that's difficult to reach.

1

2

Avoiding damage

A bungled harbour manoeuvre can be saved if the fenders are at the ready; otherwise, it may require determined intervention by hand. There are certain rules with regard to safety and etiquette.

Fender boards

For manoeuvres at rough walls or mooring posts, such as easing against the forward spring line or when tying up at jetties with mooring posts, use a fender board as shown. It's also usually necessary where you need to avoid contact with the hull of the boat and there's a danger that the fenders could slip out of place – as at a mooring post with fenders suspended crosswise.

Sailing away

All the parts of someone else's boat that are built to take weight can be used as grips for pulling your own boat closer or pushing it out of the way. Cleats are completely unproblematic **1** as is the toerail. A line can also be quickly slipped over a cleat to stop the boat drifting. Bow and stern pulpits **2** as a rule can stand a strong pull or push, and so can the shrouds **3**. They're also the most easily reached. A boathook isn't used enough in leaving and berthing manoeuvres: its length means it can make contact with the hull of the boat much sooner than a hand can. However, when pushing away always hold the shaft in front of your body, **4** otherwise there's a danger of injury or you could fall overboard if it should slip. It's more suitable as a remedy against drifting away, used either on the shrouds **5** or the pulpit **6**.

Fender trick – or fender kick

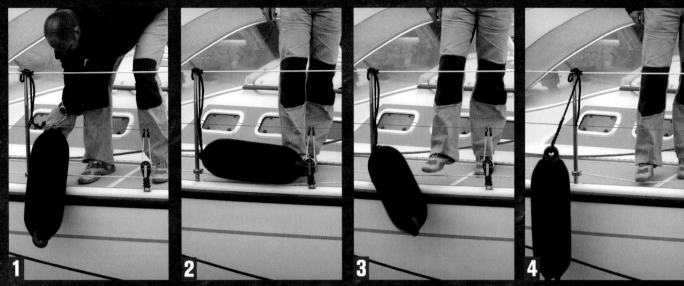

With a small crew lowering the fenders must be done quickly. There's a clever trick for doing this. **1** The fender is lowered as normal before the manoeuvre, **2** but then brought through from the outside under the lowest guardrail to lie on deck. **3** Should it now need to be lowered a kick is enough. **4** The fender slips overboard then hangs lowered as before, but it doesn't have to be lifted over the guardrail again. Where there are mooring posts a fender will only be lowered after you've passed them, to avoid it getting caught between the boat's side and a mooring post and the guardrail being dragged off.

Mind your fingers!

The guardrails **1** and stanchions are the most tempting for support and tying up **4** because they're the most easily reached. However, no owner likes to see that and there's a danger of injury from wire strands. And you should never grab hold over the guardrail **2** as that can lead to grazes. If the boathook is used like this **3** it can be become like a lance: very dangerous! Pushing away with the feet is also a problem, as shown here **5** and **6**. Anyone who slips while doing this or who hasn't correctly calculated the room needed to manoeuvre won't be able to move back or get out of the way in time and risks serious injury or a fall.

Important knots

A few knots are important for tying up and for harbour and anchor manoeuvres. Here are short instructions for the most important.

Reef knot

This is used to join two lines with the same circumference and made of the same material, for example both working ends of the same line. It holds reliably so long as tension is put on it, and is easily undone by pulling on one of the ends.

Both working ends cross over one another and then cross over again. The working end which was on top at the beginning must be on top again. Pull all four strands tight.

Double sheet bend

The alternative to a reef knot if ropes of different sizes have to be joined, such as a flag's line to a halyard. The sheet bend holds more firmly the more load there is on it.

Work from the bottom to the top through and around the loop. Pass the working end of the line through (a simple sheet bend) and then do the same thing once more.

Clove hitch around an object

It's the standard knot for securing a fender to the guardrail. (A fender can also be secured with two half hitches.)

Pass the working end away from you over the wire from the top to the bottom and then from the bottom to the top, so that the working end passes under the wire through the loop that's been formed.

Clove hitch over a post

This variation is very good for tying up to a bollard, as when laying a spring line, or to prevent a loop from riding up. The whole line mustn't be pulled through. If the working end isn't under tension at the end, secure it with a half hitch.

Make two turns so that the working end lies on top of one and under the other. Slide them over each other, then pass them over the pole and pull tight.

Figure of eight

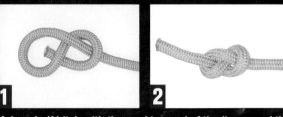

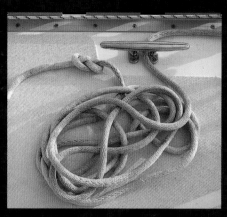

A figure of eight holds securely, but can be undone easily. It's used to stop the working end of the line being pulled through an eye or cleat, as here with the mooring line and cleat.

Make a half hitch with the working end of the line round the standing end and push the working end through the loop from the back.

Rolling hitch

When pulled in the directions shown the knot doesn't slip on the (white) line and will also hold on stays, shrouds and handrails. This way tow lines can be attached to a central hawser or a pennant to a shroud. It is very useful for releasing a sheet by taking the strain off it. It only holds when pulled in the direction in which the two round turns lie, and slips in the other direction. The line being attached should be thinner than the other one.

To attach the yellow line to the white, pass the working end of the yellow line around the white line twice, then across itself and make a reverse round turn and pull the working end through.

Bowline

The bowline is the most reliable knot for making a loop in a line. It also holds during load changes as in tying up, but is still easily undone without having to pull too hard. It can be used to join two lines – as when towing – by tying a bowline in each line so that the loops interlock.

Form a loop with the working end, then pass the working end through that loop from underneath, round the standing end and push through the loop again. Pull on the standing end of the line.

Round turn and two half hitches

This knot is an alternative to a bowline when you want to attach a mooring line to a ring on the jetty. The advantage over a bowline when tying up is that there's a great deal of friction after both round turns have been made, which is important for a mooring line under load. In addition it's very easy to remember how to tie it!

Thread the working end twice through the ring or object, then tie two half hitches.

Manoeuvring with the engine

Today it's normal to use the engine when manoeuvring, thanks to its high reliability. But even though this makes it much easier, there is no standard manoeuvre: a great deal depends on the conditions. Since these are never the same, there is theoretically an endless number of variations on tying up and sailing away.

Nowhere is it written that a mooring manoeuvre has to be elegant. The main consideration is that your own and other people's boats should come out of it intact. One of the easiest ways of achieving this is to go about it slowly and carefully: that way you have the best chance of correcting any mistakes. But a strong wind or current can take you off course or make it necessary to keep the speed of the boat relatively high so that it remains manoeuvrable. In addition modern boats with short keels, as explained earlier, have a great tendency to drift, unlike long keelers. They really need to be manoeuvred at speed in a strong wind, because greater speed through the water produces directional stability and stops you drifting off course. This lessens the danger of serious damage.

An alternative to this is to travel slowly remembering the older virtues, like the use of manoeuvring lines. These not only give more security, but properly positioned they can help to avoid unnecessarily high loads on ropes, which is particularly important for small or weak crews.

Achieving a reasonable balance between motor and muscle power requires a little basic knowledge. This includes on the one hand knowing how the boat behaves under widely differing conditions. The following pages provide help on knowing how to assess the behaviour of a boat. This is particularly important for charterers, who quite naturally may know very little about their floating saucers.

Also included in this basic knowledge is knowing how these conditions generally might appear. Anyone approaching an unknown harbour should have previously obtained information about specific features. Are you tying up to a jetty with mooring posts

or using a Mediterranean moor, do you have to take into account the current or a strong wind, is the anchor needed or will you possibly have to head for an anchorage which can only be reached with difficulty? The relevant harbour handbook will give you most of the answers, and the skipper should have drawn up some sort of plan of action prior to getting there: where is the anchorage you want, what alternatives are there, which areas are to be avoided?

In the final analysis, choosing the right manoeuvre must generally be carried out on the spot. Since the skipper can be under great pressure for this reason, not to mention the high volume of traffic or the very restricted space for manoeuvre, the basic procedures have to be practised again and again so that they become automatic. This chapter offers assistance to help achieve that.

Starting and stopping

It's important to know how the boat reacts when stationary. If there's propeller walk does the flow go directly over the rudder? From a standing start give a burst on the engine with the rudder amidships, and observe the reaction. When the boat reaches a speed of three or four knots, stop with full throttle astern, and leave the gearbox for a little while to adjust. Observe the reaction again. If the stern breaks away, how long is the run-out X?

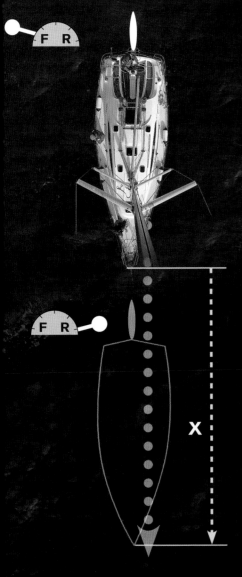

Going astern and prop walk

Prop walk can be used to help many manoeuvres. Depending on the kind of drive this can be strong or weak: stronger for boats with a propshaft and fixed pitch propeller, weaker for those with a Sail-drive (because the propeller lies closer to the keel and the centre of rotation of the boat and consequently there's less leverage available). The shape of the hull also plays a role. It's also important to know which way the propeller turns when going ahead and going astern. This is usually indicated by an arrow on the gearbox. No matter how clearly marked this is, it can best be tested by going full astern from stationary. If the stern breaks away as in the diagram on the left, you have to go with the flow. Then as soon as the boat has picked up speed you can usually bring it back into the desired direction with the rudder. Prop walk can best be explained by an illustration such as the one below. You have to imagine the propeller turning like a wheel over the bottom and taking the stern of the boat with it. Here the engine is going astern so the propeller, as on most modern boats, turns anticlockwise and the stern kicks to port.

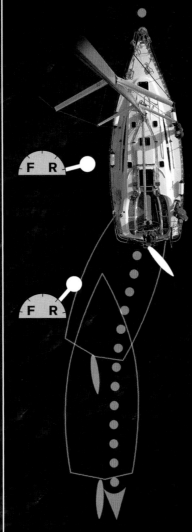

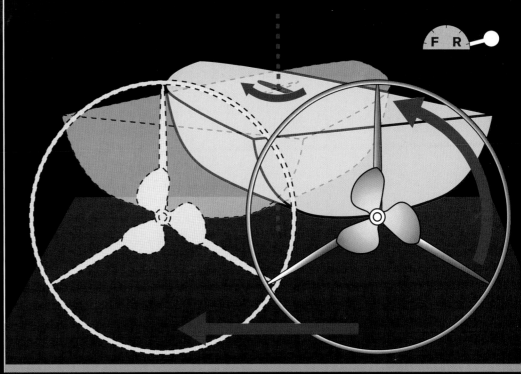

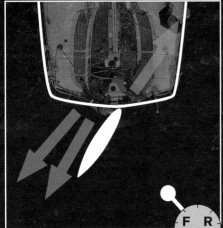
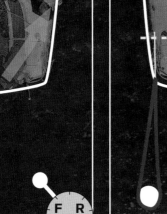
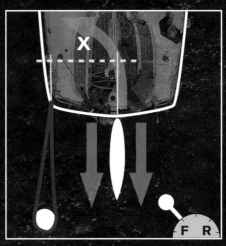

Current

Boats are steered at the stern. When going ahead the wash from the propeller pushes against the line of the rudder blade. This produces resistance through pressure on the blade and the whole stern turns with it. Therefore it's also possible to manoeuvre when the boat is stationary. Instead of current coming from the speed of the boat, the current comes from the propeller. The closer this is to the rudder blade, the stronger the current.

Leverage

A boat can also be manoeuvred on the spot by using one of the forward, midship or aft spring lines – these are described in detail on the following pages. They can also be manoeuvred by a line over the stern, which works particularly well with modern wide sterns. As you can see in the diagram a pivot forms through the transverse distance X between the propeller and the point of action of the stern line, which causes the boat to swing to port.

Combining current and leverage

Used correctly, the current on the rudder blade and the leverage effect on the stern can help to make amazing manoeuvres possible, such as the one described on p. 25. In the example shown here the boat would turn to port very quickly. But it could also hold its position with the rudder to starboard, because then both effects are working against each other. In all three examples the strength of the effect can be controlled through forward bursts on the motor.

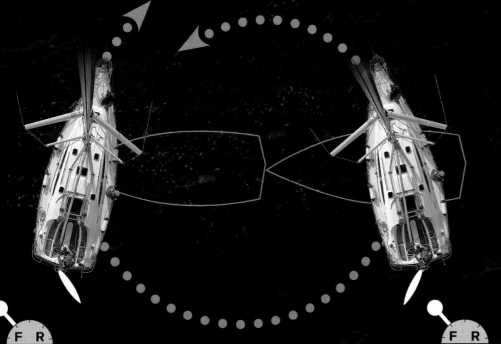
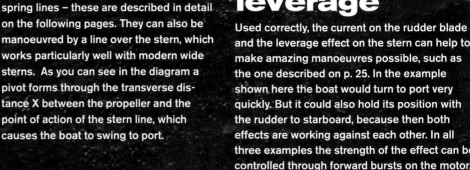

Full circles

You often have to turn in narrow channels, or take evasive action. Then the skipper must know how much space the boat needs for turning. You can easily find this out before entering the harbour by doing a couple of trial circles. When you do this you have to know whether to take prop effect into account as described above. For a propeller that turns clockwise the stern of the boat will move to starboard when going ahead which assists turning to port and makes for a smaller circle than when turning to starboard. To measure the full circle turn the rudder fully and remember that every circle can be varied by bursts on the motor. A diameter of one to two boat's lengths is normal for a modern short keeler; for long keelers it can come to many times more than that.

Leaving a jetty with the leverage effect

If a manoeuvre at a jetty with mooring posts goes wrong it quite often ends in a lee shore situation and a rescue mission along the mooring posts – which is a bit like running the gauntlet. The boat brushes against every mooring post and with luck eventually frees herself. Modern boats with their wide sterns open up possibilities for manoeuvring which would have been unthinkable before. Because the cleat is a long way from the centreline, it acts as a long lever arm. If this is used correctly, and using the thrust of a modern engine, it brings many dangerous situations such as this one under control. The boat is propelled almost sideways off the mooring posts. It can now be freed by easing against the forward spring line. To do this, however, you have to change gear and fender well. The same goes for easing against the after spring line. Both manoeuvres when sailing away from a jetty are described on pp. 94 and 95. However, the manoeuvre described here has the advantage of greater control over the boat, and in addition you don't need to have fenders in place while doing it. STERN LINES ARE ALSO USEFUL WHEN DOCKING BETWEEN PILES AND A JETTY – SEE THE NEXT PAGE

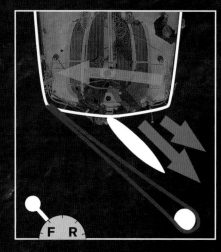

Because the rudder is over to starboard the stern is pulled to port. Because the boat is pushing against the mooring line at the same time the bow turns to port. So the boat settles parallel to the mooring posts, an ideal compromise between two laws of physics.

WIND

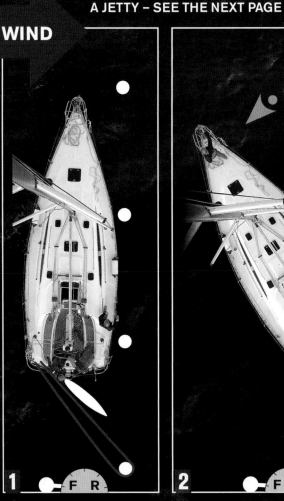

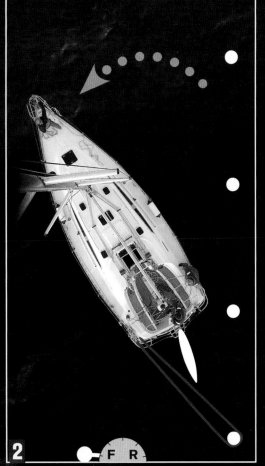

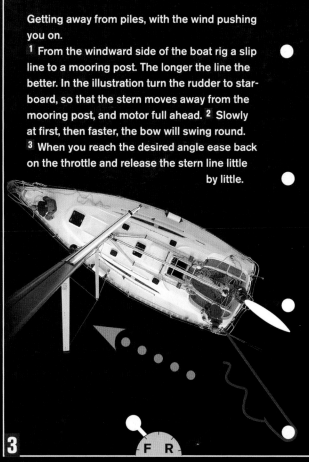

Getting away from piles, with the wind pushing you on.
[1] From the windward side of the boat rig a slip line to a mooring post. The longer the line the better. In the illustration turn the rudder to starboard, so that the stern moves away from the mooring post, and motor full ahead. [2] Slowly at first, then faster, the bow will swing round. [3] When you reach the desired angle ease back on the throttle and release the stern line little by little.

1

2

3

WIND

3 With an offshore wind like this you can motor straight into the berth, with a crosswind hold the bow a little to windward.

4 The boat motors slowly ahead. On each side the crew lays a loop of the stern mooring line over a mooring post.

2 Deciding when you have reached the right point for swinging into the mooring place depends very much on the type of boat and her manoeuvrability. You should be able to establish this with the method described at the beginning. You also have to take wind strength and direction into account. Anyone who is unsure should move the rudder rather earlier than planned. Better the boat ends up going diagonally into the berth than carrying on past the mooring posts.

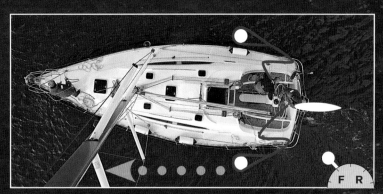

5 The crew and/or the helmsman hold the slack of the stern lines in the cockpit, and the bow line is held ready in the bow.

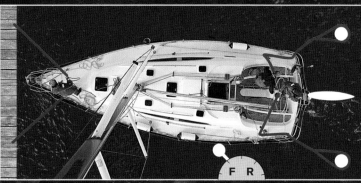

6 Stop about a metre away from the jetty and tighten the stern mooring lines. Immediately afterwards give a little more forwards thrust again. The boat can easily be held against a crosswind through the leverage effect on the leeward mooring line. When stopping under power there is a danger that the stern will turn away because of the prop effect. Therefore the boat can also be stopped by sensitively using the mooring lines round the winches. Then by paying out slowly the boat can be brought close to the jetty and the bow lines attached to the jetty.

1 One person stands at the bow and keeps a lookout for a vacant mooring place. This will give the helmsman more time to react.

Direct entry

You can turn the boat into a berth if the mooring lane is wide enough to allow a 90-degree turn without a problem and if the wind is light to moderate. The berth should also be long enough to be able to slow down using the stern lines, that is, at least two metres longer than the hull. For a crew of three or more the method (left, p26) is recommended. It's also suitable in a stronger offshore or onshore wind. If there's a strong crosswind the method (right) is a variation which is also suitable for a two-man crew or a single-handed sailor. But both variations have a disadvantage: if you don't manage to secure the stern line correctly at the first attempt, getting it right at the second attempt is more difficult. Therefore a further alternative is shown on the next page. Entering an anchorage should always take place as far to windward as possible in a crosswind. That secures manoeuvring space to leeward, which can be particularly important in a strong wind (the situation on p. 34 shows an exception). If the wind is blowing parallel to the lane the entry should always take place into the wind, otherwise the situations described on the following pages can arise. Part of the preparation for tying up at a mooring post is that there should of course be four mooring lines, two at the bow and two at the stern. The stern lines should be equipped with loops which are brought forward on the outside of the boat to the widest place. That way they can be laid more easily over the mooring posts. Secure the mooring lines against slipping!

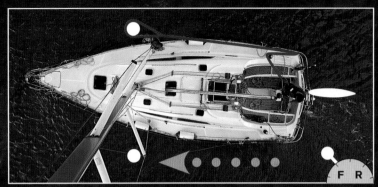

4 You will have approached as in steps 1–3 opposite. Motor close to the windward mooring post. Lay the windward stern mooring rope over it. A single-handed sailor does this from the cockpit.

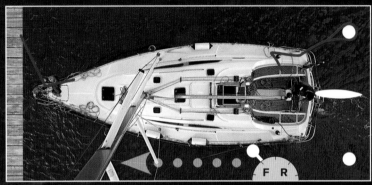

5 Use the stern line to stop the boat just before the jetty and ease in against the stern line. Make the windward bow line fast.

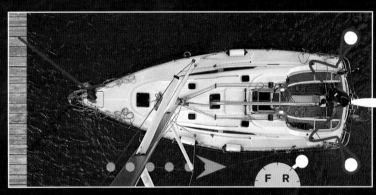

6 Motor astern go astern. Keep the bow lines and the windward stern lines under tension. Attach the leeward, aft mooring line.

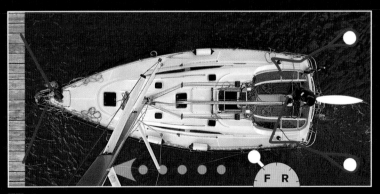

7 Ease forward against both stern lines, paying them out slowly. Then make the leeward bow line fast.

Using a midship spring line in a short mooring space

A midship cleat (or a lip cleat over which a mooring line can be taken) gives the option of many different manoeuvres like the one here. If the mooring space is very short, so that you can't stop the boat with the stern lines, a midship spring line lengthens the braking distance. But above all it's the method of choice when there's such a strong crosswind that you have to take into account a strong sideways drift. When easing against a midship spring line the bow miraculously allows itself to hold to windward, and indeed even the whole boat if the rudder is over a little to the leeward side, for this also moves the stern to windward as explained earlier. In addition to two bow and stern lines you should also have ready a line amidships. This is brought back from the outside into the cockpit, particularly when the crew is small, so that from there it can be taken round the winch so the helmsman can adjust it.

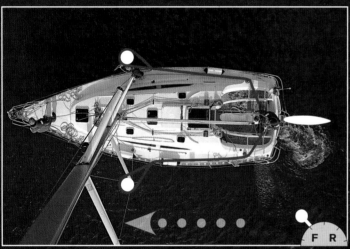

1 As soon as you can reach the mooring posts, make fast both midship spring lines. Meanwhile the boat runs slowly into the berth.

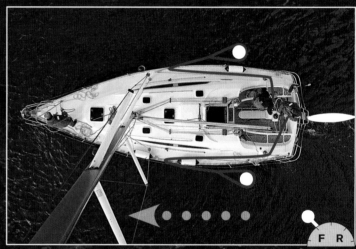

2 Just after the midship cleats have passed the mooring posts tension the midship spring lines on their winches.

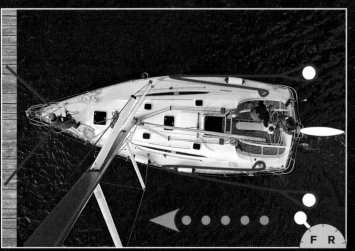

3 When the boat has stopped pay out the midship spring lines and adjust the boat with the rudder position and thrust. Make fast the bow lines.

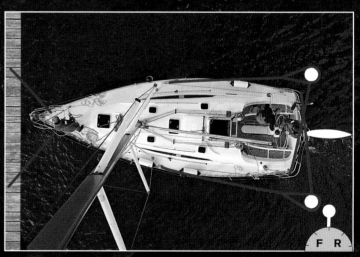

4 Fix the midship spring lines; they remain on the mooring posts astern as security. Rig crossed stern lines as shown.

Midship spring lines with a small crew

Let's look at a variation on the manoeuvre described on page 28 for a two-man crew (and it's also good for a single-handed sailor). In position (2) of our new sequence the skipper can adjust the boat very skilfully with thrust and rudder position, or he can rig a stern line to leeward, then ease against the midship spring line and the stern line, establish equilibrium and rig a bow line to windward. Whatever the case, the boat is secured on the windward side.

1 Run into the mooring place on the windward side so that a crew member can lay the windward midship spring line over the mooring post.

3 Bring the boat to the jetty by paying out the midship spring line and motoring ahead. The bowman rigs the bow line to windward.

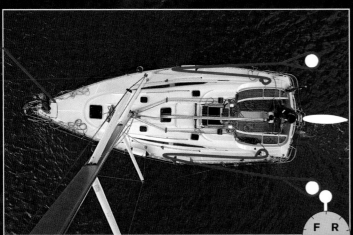

2 The helmsman takes over the midship spring line. As soon as the midship cleat has passed the mooring post, he tightens the line. The boat stops.

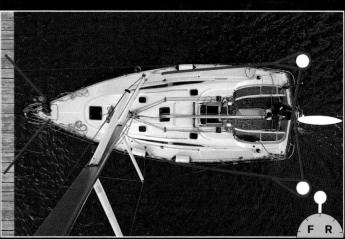

4 Bring the boat a little astern again, rig the other midship spring line, then tighten the spring lines.

5 Rig the leeward bow line and two mooring lines astern to secure the boat crosswise. Adjust all the lines to position the boat properly.

WIND

Bringing the boat under control with a bow line

The skipper has tried to steer into the berth with the wind astern! Particularly as a result of the bow being blown downwind the turning circle has unexpectedly increased considerably, and the mooring place has been missed. This phenomenon also occurs as a result of a current in the same direction as the wind. It would have been better to have approached the berth against the wind. Now it's important to secure the boat with a line.

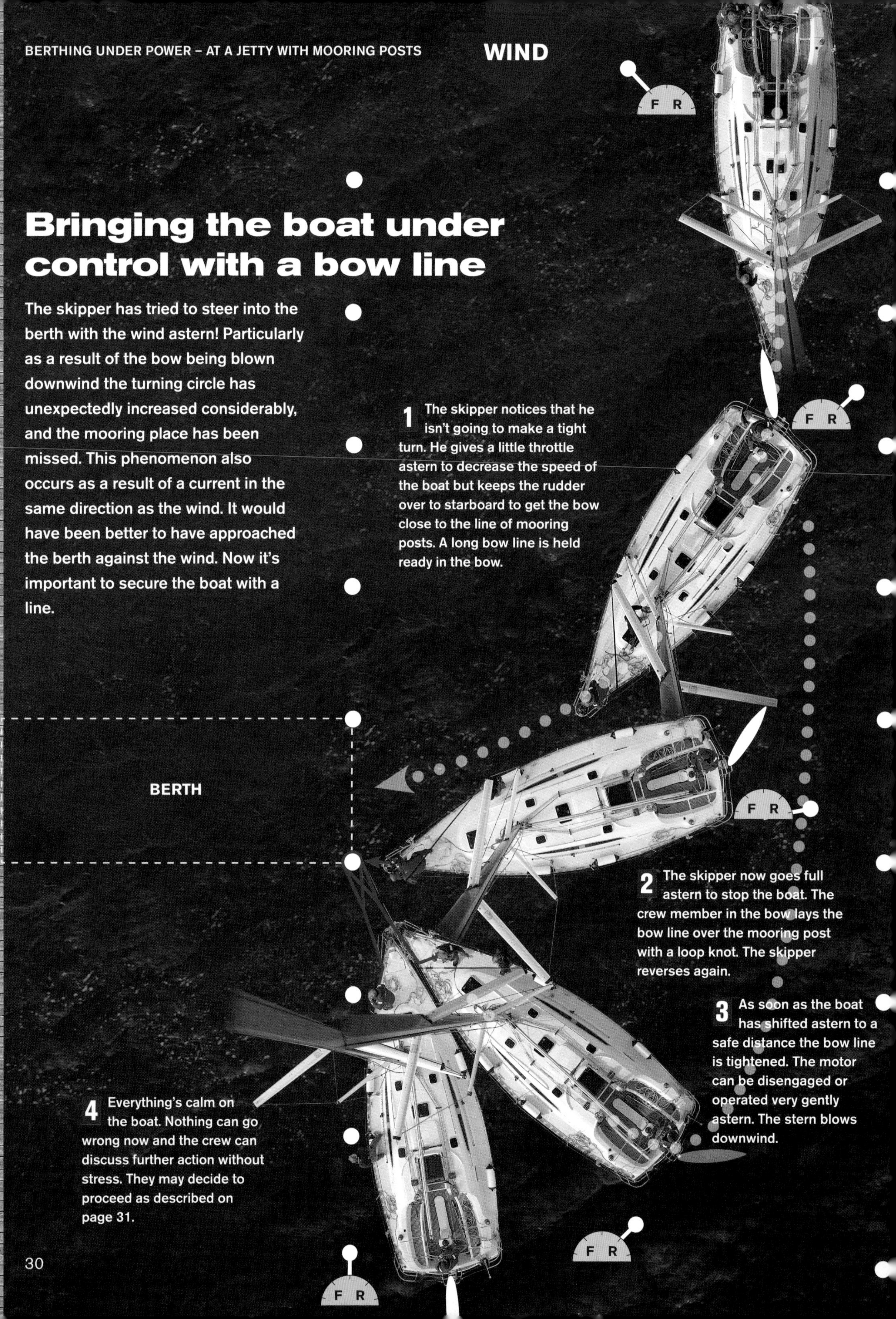

1 The skipper notices that he isn't going to make a tight turn. He gives a little throttle astern to decrease the speed of the boat but keeps the rudder over to starboard to get the bow close to the line of mooring posts. A long bow line is held ready in the bow.

BERTH

2 The skipper now goes full astern to stop the boat. The crew member in the bow lays the bow line over the mooring post with a loop knot. The skipper reverses again.

3 As soon as the boat has shifted astern to a safe distance the bow line is tightened. The motor can be disengaged or operated very gently astern. The stern blows downwind.

4 Everything's calm on the boat. Nothing can go wrong now and the crew can discuss further action without stress. They may decide to proceed as described on page 31.

Using forward and midship spring lines to berth

The boat is currently attached to the leeward stern mooring post of the berth into which the skipper now wants to steer. He could let the boat drift astern and have another go at turning into the berth. That would actually be easier than with the wind astern, but it would run the risk of missing the mooring place again or ending up wedged diagonally between the mooring posts. In addition, in a strong wind, it may be dangerous to untie the only line that is holding the boat. In the manoeuvre shown here the boat is always under control. This can also be carried out by a two-man crew. Alternatively the midship spring line can be fed around a winch and taken to the helmsman.

1 If necessary, lower fenders on the port side. Move the boat ahead to the mooring post. The bow line, now a spring line, is paid out over the cleat in a controlled manner by the person in the bow. When you've almost reached the starboard mooring post, make this forward spring line fast. Rudder hard to port, motor ahead.

2 As soon as the bow has passed the mooring post, pay out the forward spring line again slowly. Now secure a midship spring line to starboard and keep it tight in a controlled manner (this also works with a bow spring line, p. 33).

3 As soon as the midship cleat to starboard has passed the mooring post, the midship spring line is paid out in a controlled manner by the helmsman.

4 Untie the port forward spring line and secure it as a stern line. When you reach the jetty secure the bow lines.

WIND

1 The helmsman notices early that he's going to miss the berth. By throttling back hard he reduces the speed of the boat, but lets the boat run on long enough to position her bow just in front of the row of mooring posts. That creates space to manoeuvre as the bow blows downwind.

4 Once you've reached the mooring posts of the berth you want, establish calm in the boat. Enter the berth if you can, otherwise, as here, attach a stern line to the post, make the boat fast, let your pulse rate go down – then think what to do next (see facing page).

BERTH

Bringing the boat under control with a stern line

The starting point is the same as on p. 30. The berth has been missed, with the wind astern. But apart from making the bow fast to a mooring post there is a second chance to rescue the manoeuvre. The skipper uses the weathervane effect of modern boats, which is the way the bow blows downwind faster than the stern.

This kind of approach is often better anyway, because you can motor forwards out of the lane in the event of there not being a free space.

2 With the throttle in neutral or a gentle forward thrust the helmsman waits until the wind has turned the bow. He lets the boat drift to leeward but keeps the space to the row of mooring posts to starboard as large as possible.

3 Now he applies full throttle astern, with the rudder hard to starboard. With a propshaft that turns clockwise ease off the revs when the boat has picked up speed. Prop walk would otherwise pull the stern against the row of mooring posts.

Turning with a forward spring line and stern line

The boat, which on the facing page was tied up to the mooring post by the stern after the unsuccessful approach to the berth, has swung stern to the wind. She's lying across the berth, whereas we want the bow into the berth. The forward spring line is useful in this situation too. The boat is turned so the stern passes through the wind, which then does most of the work. The manoeuvre depends on good co-ordination between the helmsman and the bowman. Of course, you may need fenders to protect the boat from the posts.

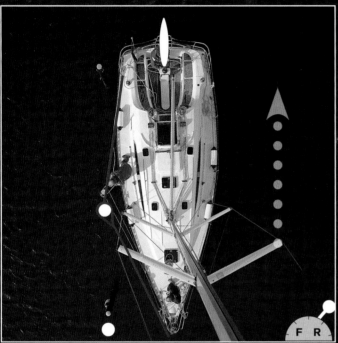

1 Pull the boat astern under power. As soon as possible lay the forward spring line over the starboard mooring post of the berth. If the bow has passed the port mooring post of the berth, tighten the forward spring. Meanwhile pay out the stern line in a controlled manner.

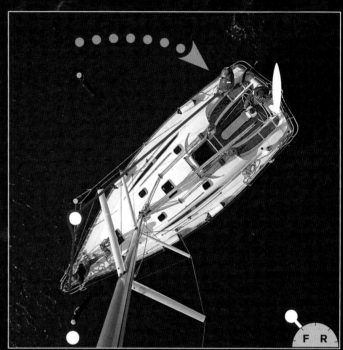

2 Push the rudder to starboard and go half ahead – the stern begins to turn. The helmsman controls the speed of the turn with the rudder position and the throttle. He can stop the turn with port rudder and more revs.

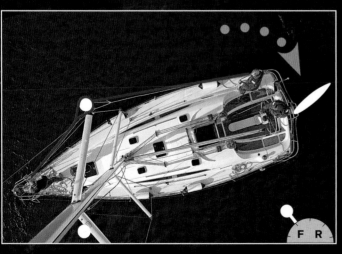

3 Pay out the forward spring line slowly, hold the slack of the stern line. If it's very windy fend off the leeward mooring post.

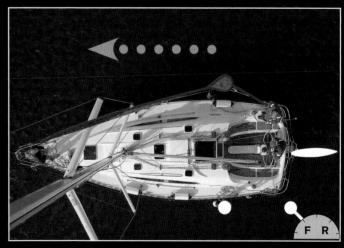

4 The wind is pushing the stern onto the leeward mooring post. This can be counteracted with a port rudder and the engine full ahead.

4 The helmsman brings the bow to the next mooring post past the berth and stops. The bowman secures a bow line to it and the stern aligns itself with the wind direction. The boat is secured, the danger averted.

WIND

3 The boat drifts completely past the berth. Again, the first goal is to establish a secure a line to shore or to a mooring post. Otherwise, in a narrow lane and with a crosswind there's a great danger of drifting into the row of mooring posts and getting stuck there.

2 The crew member at the bow sees a free berth and signals this to the helmsman. He reacts too late, calculates the crosswind wrongly or simply doesn't have enough time to bring the bow between the two chosen mooring posts.

1 Because he knows he is going to have to turn left, the helmsman motors along the right-hand side of the lane. (This has the disadvantage that there's no room left for manoeuvring to leeward.)

5 Instead of letting go the bow line and sailing freely into the berth, which would also be possible, the skipper decides to keep attached to the current post. The short bow line is replaced by a long manoeuvring line, arranged as a slip line around the post and back to the boat.

WIND

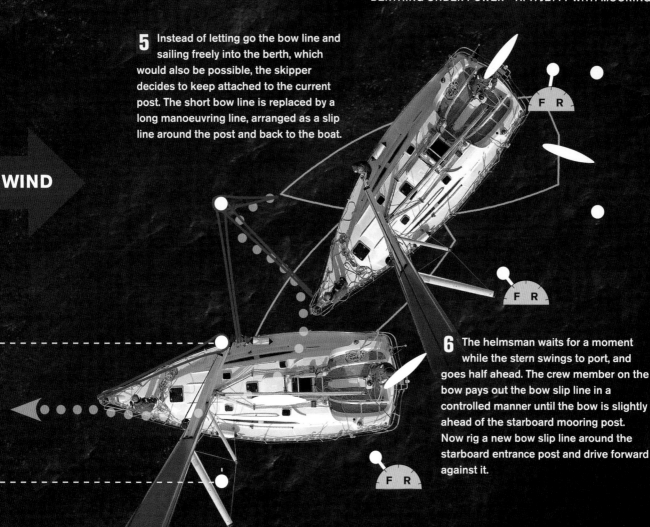

6 The helmsman waits for a moment while the stern swings to port, and goes half ahead. The crew member on the bow pays out the bow slip line in a controlled manner until the bow is slightly ahead of the starboard mooring post. Now rig a new bow slip line around the starboard entrance post and drive forward against it.

7 The helmsman controls the angle of entry through the position of the rudder and the use of the throttle. As soon as half the boat has entered the berth the stern lines can be attached. Then the forward spring line is untied and hauled in. Just a little more throttle ahead and you're done!

Forward spring line over two mooring posts

On board, apart from the usual four mooring lines, there should also at least be one additional manoeuvring line three times the length of the boat. Amazing manoeuvres can be accomplished with its help. It should float, so that when throwing it out and hauling it in it can't foul the propeller.

In this example the wind is blowing out of the berth, more or less offshore. The bow is pushed to leeward and the turning circle increases. In a very narrow lane the turning manoeuvre won't work.

WIND

3 The wind finishes the job: the stern swings around, the helmsman puts the rudder hard to port.
As soon as the correct angle is achieved, just give a burst ahead on the motor with the rudder amidships, and the boat will glide into the berth.

4 The bowman slips the bow line from the port mooring post. Incidentally, if the first mooring post had been passed, the second (starboard) post would have done just as well for the same manoeuvre.

2 The person posted on the bow locates a free space, and gives hand signals to the helmsman. The helmsman takes a bearing on the first mooring post, and stops. The bowman secures a bow line to the mooring post with a slip rope. The helmsman now motors gently astern.

1 This is another way of getting into the same berth, with the same offshore wind. This time the helmsman motors along the left-hand side of the lane, i.e. keeps to windward. In this way he gains a great deal of room to leeward.

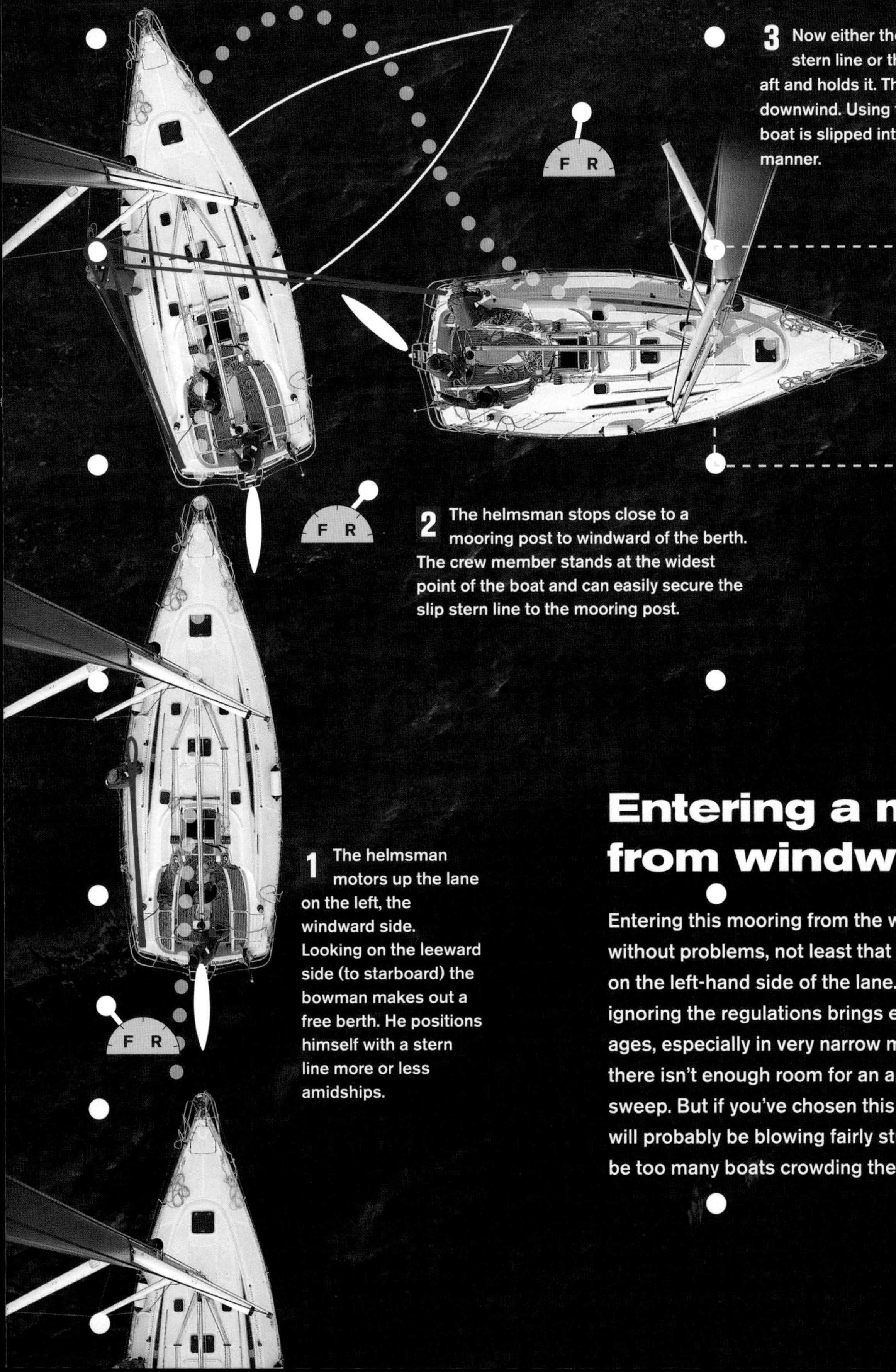

WIND

3 Now either the helmsman holds the stern line or the crew member moves aft and holds it. The wind pushes the bow downwind. Using the long stern line the boat is slipped into the berth in a controlled manner.

F R

F R

2 The helmsman stops close to a mooring post to windward of the berth. The crew member stands at the widest point of the boat and can easily secure the slip stern line to the mooring post.

1 The helmsman motors up the lane on the left, the windward side. Looking on the leeward side (to starboard) the bowman makes out a free berth. He positions himself with a stern line more or less amidships.

F R

Entering a mooring from windward

Entering this mooring from the windward side is not without problems, not least that you have to motor on the left-hand side of the lane. But for once ignoring the regulations brings enormous advantages, especially in very narrow mooring lanes where there isn't enough room for an approach in a large sweep. But if you've chosen this method the wind will probably be blowing fairly strongly so there won't be too many boats crowding the lane.

Approaching stern first

If the mooring lane is very narrow or the skipper is worried that he will have difficulty turning (see page 82), it's better to approach stern first. This works well with a short-keeled boat since, unlike a long keeler, she can be steered astern very well. You just have to be careful that the rudder doesn't swing hard over. The other disadvantage is that you can't sail into the berth in one go, at least not if the bow has to be pointing to the jetty, as is usual in northern regions.

WIND

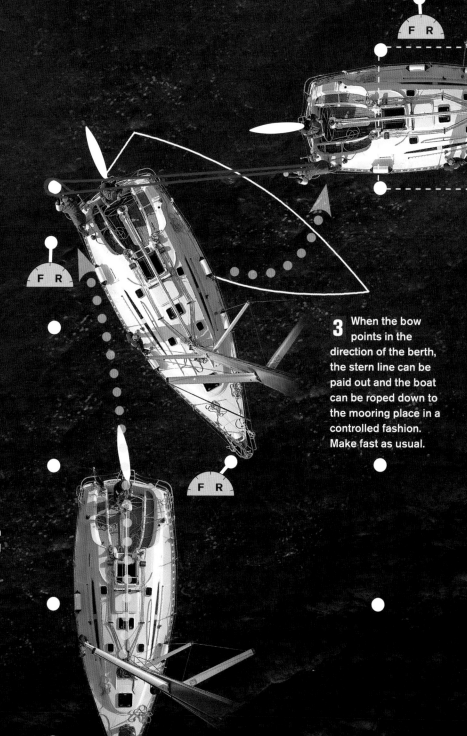

2 Stop and rig a slip line to a mooring post on the opposite side from the mooring you're heading for. The wind now blows the bow slowly downwind.

3 When the bow points in the direction of the berth, the stern line can be paid out and the boat can be roped down to the mooring place in a controlled fashion. Make fast as usual.

1 The helmsman reverses the boat along the windward side of the mooring lane. That has the advantage that you still have room to manoeuvre when stopping, if the bow starts to drift. This method is recommended for single-handed sailors since, if the approach is unsuccessful, they can approach a mooring post with the stern and don't have to go far from the wheel and the gear lever when making fast with the stern line.

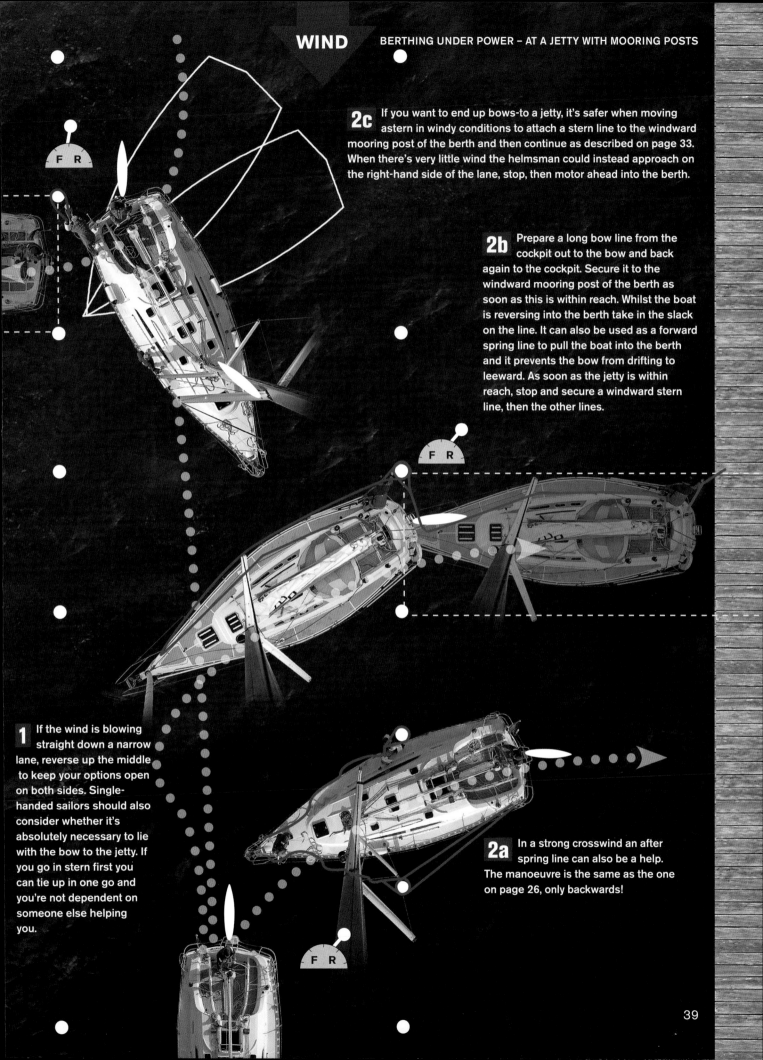

2c If you want to end up bows-to a jetty, it's safer when moving astern in windy conditions to attach a stern line to the windward mooring post of the berth and then continue as described on page 33. When there's very little wind the helmsman could instead approach on the right-hand side of the lane, stop, then motor ahead into the berth.

2b Prepare a long bow line from the cockpit out to the bow and back again to the cockpit. Secure it to the windward mooring post of the berth as soon as this is within reach. Whilst the boat is reversing into the berth take in the slack on the line. It can also be used as a forward spring line to pull the boat into the berth and it prevents the bow from drifting to leeward. As soon as the jetty is within reach, stop and secure a windward stern line, then the other lines.

1 If the wind is blowing straight down a narrow lane, reverse up the middle to keep your options open on both sides. Single-handed sailors should also consider whether it's absolutely necessary to lie with the bow to the jetty. If you go in stern first you can tie up in one go and you're not dependent on someone else helping you.

2a In a strong crosswind an after spring line can also be a help. The manoeuvre is the same as the one on page 26, only backwards!

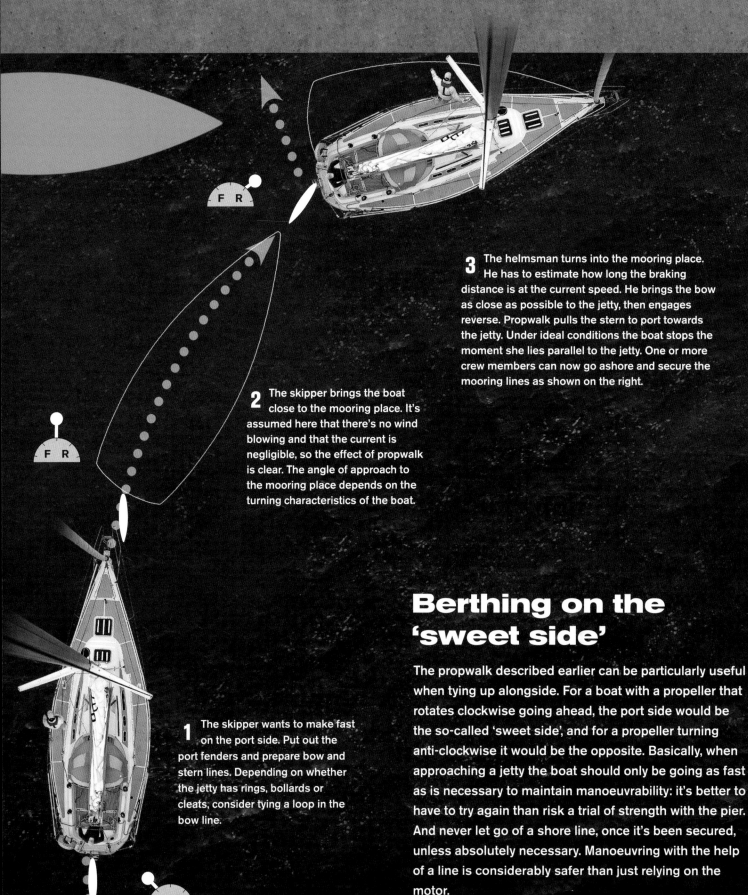

3 The helmsman turns into the mooring place. He has to estimate how long the braking distance is at the current speed. He brings the bow as close as possible to the jetty, then engages reverse. Propwalk pulls the stern to port towards the jetty. Under ideal conditions the boat stops the moment she lies parallel to the jetty. One or more crew members can now go ashore and secure the mooring lines as shown on the right.

2 The skipper brings the boat close to the mooring place. It's assumed here that there's no wind blowing and that the current is negligible, so the effect of propwalk is clear. The angle of approach to the mooring place depends on the turning characteristics of the boat.

1 The skipper wants to make fast on the port side. Put out the port fenders and prepare bow and stern lines. Depending on whether the jetty has rings, bollards or cleats, consider tying a loop in the bow line.

Berthing on the 'sweet side'

The propwalk described earlier can be particularly useful when tying up alongside. For a boat with a propeller that rotates clockwise going ahead, the port side would be the so-called 'sweet side', and for a propeller turning anti-clockwise it would be the opposite. Basically, when approaching a jetty the boat should only be going as fast as is necessary to maintain manoeuvrability: it's better to have to try again than risk a trial of strength with the pier. And never let go of a shore line, once it's been secured, unless absolutely necessary. Manoeuvring with the help of a line is considerably safer than just relying on the motor.

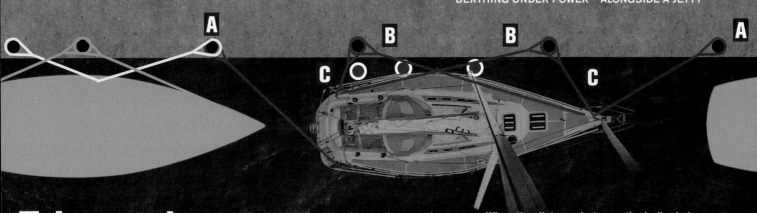

Tying up to a jetty

Maximum fendering is the overriding requirement. Jetties can be rough, with bits of rusty iron or other nasties sticking out of them. Put out everything that can be used to protect the hull. Have a fender board ready for lowering, because jetties often have mooring posts. In the following examples the mooring posts are not shown, for clarity. When tying up, the forward and aft spring lines (B) are the most important lines. They take the forces that are working in the longitudinal direction and also help hold the boat to the pier. Bow and stern lines (A), on the other hand, are to ease the strain on the spring lines and absorb the turning movements. Without spring lines the boat might drift a good way down the jetty in a strong wind.

When the distance between the bollards is too long or they're inconveniently placed or when the boat is too rounded (as in the example), the spring lines can also be set as midship spring lines (yellow) or run to a bollard in the middle (green). When there's a great deal of swell or a gusty wind angular momentum can also be prevented by the breast lines (C). In an offshore wind in particular they hold the boat parallel.

Tying up in a tidal harbour

If you don't want to have to remain permanently on board in a tidal harbour (so that you can adjust the lines with the changes in the water level), long mooring lines are the answer. The longer these are, the better. The general rule of thumb is: for every metre of change in the water level, allow for a mooring line half the length of the boat. In the diagram, where the boat has to cope with a difference in height of three metres, the spring lines (B) as well as the bow and stern lines (A) are 1.5 times as long as the boat. To prevent very long mooring lines hanging loosely at high water, weights such as an anchor or something similar can be hung from the lines as riding weights. In addition, it's important to secure the mooring lines aboard with seizings so they don't slip out of the fairleads.

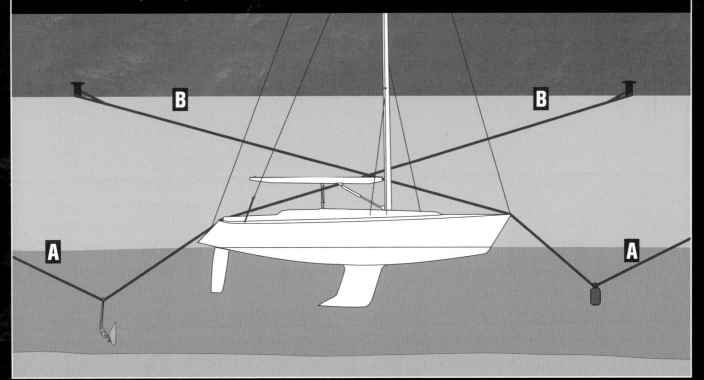

WIND

2 As soon as the quayside is within reach, the helmsman brakes with forward throttle and disengages when the boat comes to a standstill. If the rudder lies away from the pier when the motor is running, the stern will also push towards the shore. A crew member or the helmsman himself climbs over and secures the stern line as quickly as possible. Now that the boat has been secured, all the other lines can be secured at will.

1 The approach takes place stern first with just enough speed for manoeuvring. A stern line as well as a bow line are at the ready.

Using the weathervane effect

Modern short keelers can be steered astern very well, so can be brought into the wind to a mooring place in a controlled fashion. The weathervane effect (where the stern seeks the wind), described earlier, is a great help. However, the disadvantage is that the wind then blows down the companionway. The manoeuvre is also suitable for tying up against the current, providing it isn't too strong. If it is strong you will have to work against it with a great deal of thrust, and there is a danger of the rudder swinging across the boat. This manoeuvre is particularly suitable for single-handed sailors.

WIND

2 As soon as the pier is within reach, stop. A crew member goes on shore with the bow line. Until this has been secured the helmsman holds station with a gentle thrust ahead or astern. When the bow line has been made fast it holds the boat securely and the other mooring lines are then attached.

1 Approach the pier slow ahead. The interplay between approach angle and throttle is important – when it's very windy there's a danger that the bow will start to drift and may collide with the pier.

A simple way of tying up

If you're dealing with a long keeler which is difficult to steer astern, or if you want the bow to finish up pointing into the wind, then tying up bow-first into the wind is recommended. But the helmsman must be able to estimate accurately how close he can get the bow to the dock without making contact with it.

WIND

Controlling with a midship spring line

When tying up alongside, a line from amidships to the shore is very valuable. This opens up many new and extremely safe variations. The boat needs to be equipped with a central fairlead on both sides, or even better a fairlead and cleat. The midship spring line can then be brought on board and led towards the stern and over a winch and belayed. In this example, as well as the normal tying up into the wind, overcoming a cross current is shown. Using the midship spring line is also recommended in an offshore wind and on a sharp approach course.

1 Depending on the strength of the cross current or the wind the helmsman steers a course so the boat moves directly towards the required mooring place. This way narrow berths can also be reached in safety. When there's an offshore wind blowing the approach course is slightly curved.

2 Shortly before reaching the dock the helmsman swings parallel to it. A crew member secures the midship spring line directly to a bollard. As soon as the midship spring line has been secured on board, move the rudder away from the pier and run the engine half ahead.

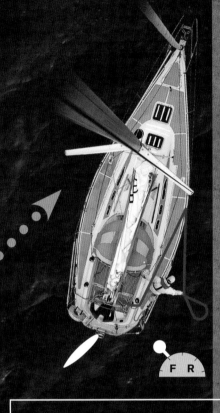

3 Because the throttle is ahead with the rudder away from the jetty the stern is pushed against it. But the leverage effect on the midship spring line tries to swing the bow towards the pier at the same time. The two effects cancel out and results in the boat lying in equilibrium, and the rest of the lines can be secured in peace and quiet.

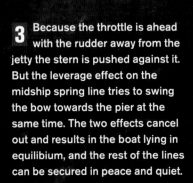

WIND

Mooring stern first using a stern line

In a strong offshore wind this manoeuvre is particularly recommended for single-handed sailors as it can be carried out stern first and the helmsman doesn't have to leave the cockpit until just before the completion of the manoeuvre. But it only works on boats with a wide stern and corresponding leverage.

1 The helmsman sets a course for one side of the mooring area and secures a stern line to the shore. Now that the boat has been secured the next step can be tackled in his own time.

WIND

Mooring stern first using a midship spring line

Like the manoeuvre described above, this is also recommended for single-handed sailors, as is every stern-first mooring. However, using the midship spring line allows an even more controlled turn than with an aft mooring line.

1 Reverse up to the pier again right into the wind. The weathervane effect helps to hold the course. As soon as a tying-up point is within reach, secure a midship spring line. A single-handed sailor must take this back into the cockpit and use it from there.

2 Give a strong burst ahead on the motor: the narrower the stern, the more the revs needed. Turn the rudder towards the pier so that the stern moves away from it, which assists the swing.

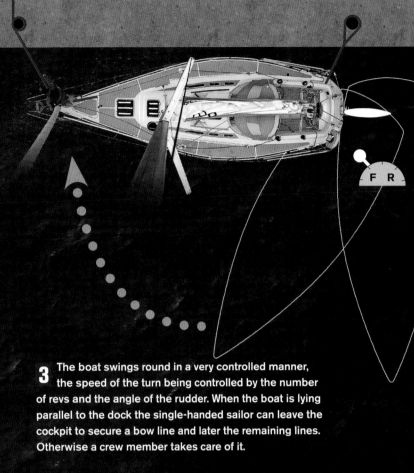

3 The boat swings round in a very controlled manner, the speed of the turn being controlled by the number of revs and the angle of the rudder. When the boat is lying parallel to the dock the single-handed sailor can leave the cockpit to secure a bow line and later the remaining lines. Otherwise a crew member takes care of it.

2 Turning the rudder towards the pier accelerates the swing, turning it away from the pier acts as a brake, both also being affected by the revs from the motor. Since the stern is moving freely here, the amount of swing can be substantially better controlled than above.

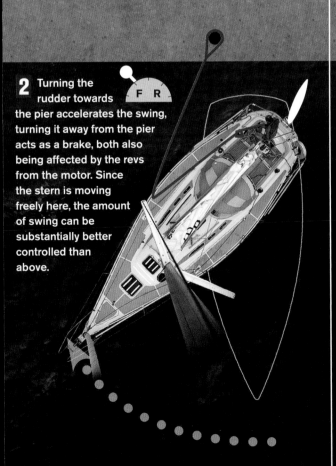

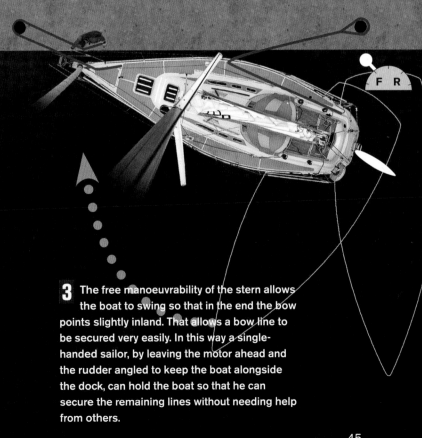

3 The free manoeuvrability of the stern allows the boat to swing so that in the end the bow points slightly inland. That allows a bow line to be secured very easily. In this way a single-handed sailor, by leaving the motor ahead and the rudder angled to keep the boat alongside the dock, can hold the boat so that he can secure the remaining lines without needing help from others.

WIND

Berthing bows first using a forward spring line

In a strong offshore wind this is a variation for boats that are difficult to manoeuvre astern, such as long keelers. Another crew member apart from the helmsman is needed, and ideally an additional helper on the shore.

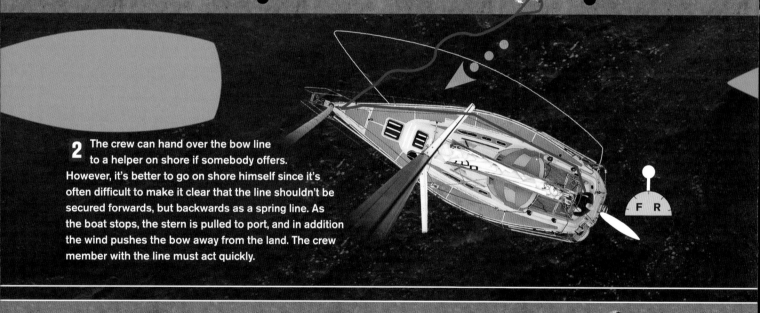

1 In this instance the approach doesn't take place on the sweet side, which makes the manoeuvre more difficult. The helmsman stops the boat just short of the dock. A crew member stands at the bow with a long bow line ready.

2 The crew can hand over the bow line to a helper on shore if somebody offers. However, it's better to go on shore himself since it's often difficult to make it clear that the line shouldn't be secured forwards, but backwards as a spring line. As the boat stops, the stern is pulled to port, and in addition the wind pushes the bow away from the land. The crew member with the line must act quickly.

3 As soon as the line is secure, the helmsman gives a burst ahead on the motor and drives against the spring line with the rudder turned away from the jetty. The boat is now under control, though the bow must be well fendered. Once a stern line has been secured the boat lies more securely. Keep the motor going gently ahead until all lines are secured.

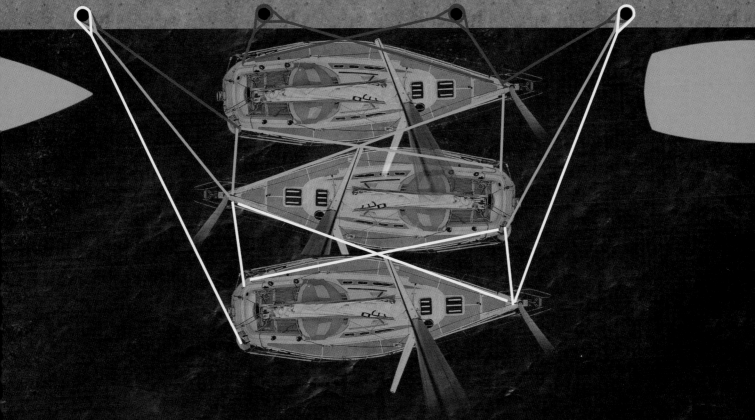

Rafting up

Lying in two or more rows is standard practice today. Tying up takes place in the same way as at a jetty, initially using a midship spring line. Ideally the smallest boat should lie on the outside, and the largest on the inside. However, this is seldom possible, and rafts build up as boats arrive. Nevertheless, in an onshore wind small boats should move to the outside since they could actually be crushed because of the enormous pressure exerted by the wind on the exposed areas of the other boats. It's also important to take care that the boats are tied up in a staggered pattern so that the rigging can't become entangled as a result of their rocking motions. This can be achieved most easily by alternating the direction each boat is heading, which also provides more privacy in the cockpits. Each boat should be tied up to the next by means of spring lines and breast lines and at the same time have her own bow line and stern line to the shore. Otherwise the innermost boat is subject to enormous shear forces in a crosswind.

Allowing her to settle

WIND

Tying up in an onshore wind is very easy because the wind does most of the work. But if it's blowing strongly the sideways drift must be slowed down to avoid damage. Lying alongside in a swell can be very unpleasant and getting away can be almost impossible.

The helmsman brings the boat as close to the jetty as possible. Once the boat has stopped the bow will blow downwind so it is sensible to position the boat with the bow into the wind a little. You have to moor here against the prop walk; the stern is moved to the jetty by a backwards burst of the motor. To slow down the rate of drift give short forward bursts of the motor, with the rudder over towards the jetty. This results in the boat swinging into the mooring area. You will need to fender well.

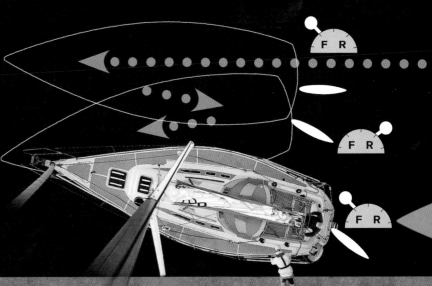

Astern into a Mediterranean moor

An approach at right angles to the mooring area is the obvious thing to do when you don't have enough room to manoeuvre, as for example in a narrow lane where there's no room to turn. It's also suitable when the wind is blowing across the mooring area since the boat is aligned like a weathervane and remains manoeuvrable at low speed. However, take care with the mooring lines of other boats, particularly in an onshore wind. If these lines are lying very flat or if the boat is drifting in a gust the keel can get caught. If you're not sure of the best time to turn towards the mooring area then use this rule of thumb: choose the moment when the your stern is more or less abeam of the bow of the last boat before the space, and put the rudder hard over.

On the other hand a straight approach is ideal in calm weather. With a slow speed astern the helmsman has enough time to adjust the trajectory of the boat to the space and correct it if necessary. This is, moreover, the correct procedure in an offshore or onshore wind. Two tips: when taking the slime line forward wear gloves if possible, since it's often muddy or has a rough surface. That's also why you shouldn't wear the clothes you'll be going ashore in! In addition: only secure a mooring line with a slip line astern for the night if you can guarantee that it won't chafe. Taking it twice round the bollard or ring cuts down on chafe, but to eliminate it altogether tie the shoreside end to the bollard.

WIND

F R

F R

A concrete block instead of an anchor

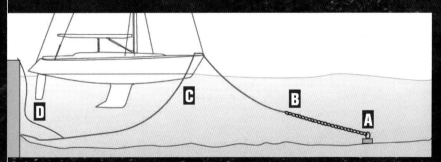

For this type of mooring you can either drop anchor and reverse towards the quay, or use a mooring buoy, or a concrete block if one has been laid. In harbours moorings frequently consist of a large block of concrete with a ring **A** . The mooring gear is tied up to this. The gear consists of a mixed cable **B** , the mooring line **C** for tying up, and frequently a very thin slime line **D** so you can pick up the mooring line from the bottom.

1 The helmsman stops short and a crew member goes ashore with the windward mooring line and makes it fast.

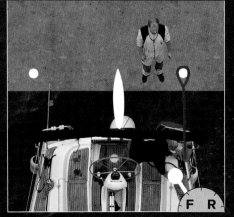

2 As soon as the mooring line has been made fast drive against it at a gentle speed ahead. The stern comes clear of the dock.

3 The bow is moved to windward through the leverage effect at the stern, and also by steering with the rudder.

4 The man on shore hauls up the mooring line from the bottom with the slime line. Sometimes the helmsman takes care of it.

5 The bowman takes over the line and works his way forward hand over hand – often a dirty job!

6 With as much strength as he can, the bowman pulls up the mooring line.

7 Secure the mooring line as quickly as possible – in a crosswind or swell huge forces can develop.

8 When everything has been done to the skipper's satisfaction, belay the mooring line with round turns and a locking turn.

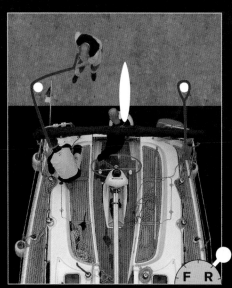

9 Re-tension the mooring line by motoring astern. Rig the leeward stern line and secure both of them.

Ahead into a Mediterranean moor

You don't always go into the mooring stern first. There are many reasons for tying up at the bow. For example, when it's not certain whether the depth of the water at the dock is sufficient for the draught of your rudder, if stones could be lying there, where the water level fluctuates or there's a possibility of swell from commercial vessels going past. Basically, when there is any danger at all of the rudder blade catching.

An exception is west-facing harbours, where tying up with the stern to the setting sun is a really nice idea. Then a sundowner tastes better in the cockpit than in the harbour bar.

There can also be a problem if the dock is very low and the bow is very high. Then gymnastic ability is necessary when getting down and getting back up.

Take care at low docks, the distance you have to jump can be enormous!

Indicating the distance to the jetty

The helmsman can have difficulty estimating distance with a low dock. Clear hand signals from the bowman can help to clarify the situation and avoid embarrassing shouting. Racing sailors also use this method on the startline.

Each finger represents one metre to the pier, plus about half a metre in reserve for safety, and the fist means stop. The countdown should start three metres away at the latest. Corrections sideways are indicated by waving the appropriate arm.

WIND

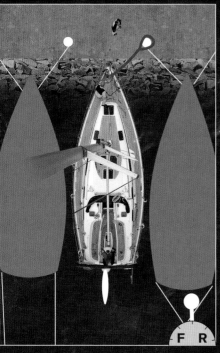

1 Motor into the mooring. Stop the boat, belay the windward bow line first and adjust so it is about one to one-and-a-half metres too long.

2 The bowman hauls in the slime line and a crew member takes it over. Keep the stern clear by careful bursts of reverse power.

3 Belay the mooring line to the stern. Prepare a second bow line.

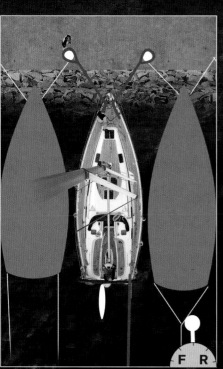

4 Secure the second bow line. The boat is now lying secure. If available, use a second mooring line to the stern.

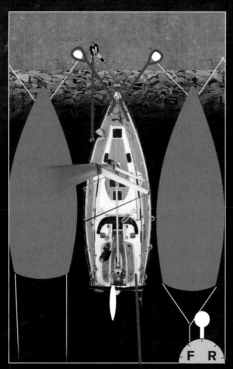

5 The bowman hauls in the second slime line from the bottom so it doesn't cross over the first, and attaches its mooring line to the other quarter.

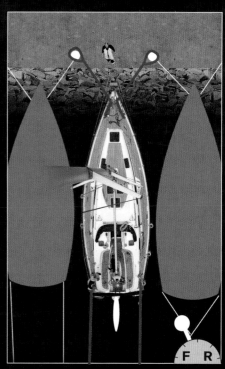

6 The helmsman drives ahead against the mooring lines and the slack on the bow lines is taken in.

If there is no block of concrete to tie up to, you will have to drop the anchor and reverse in. Pay out the anchor cable as you do so.

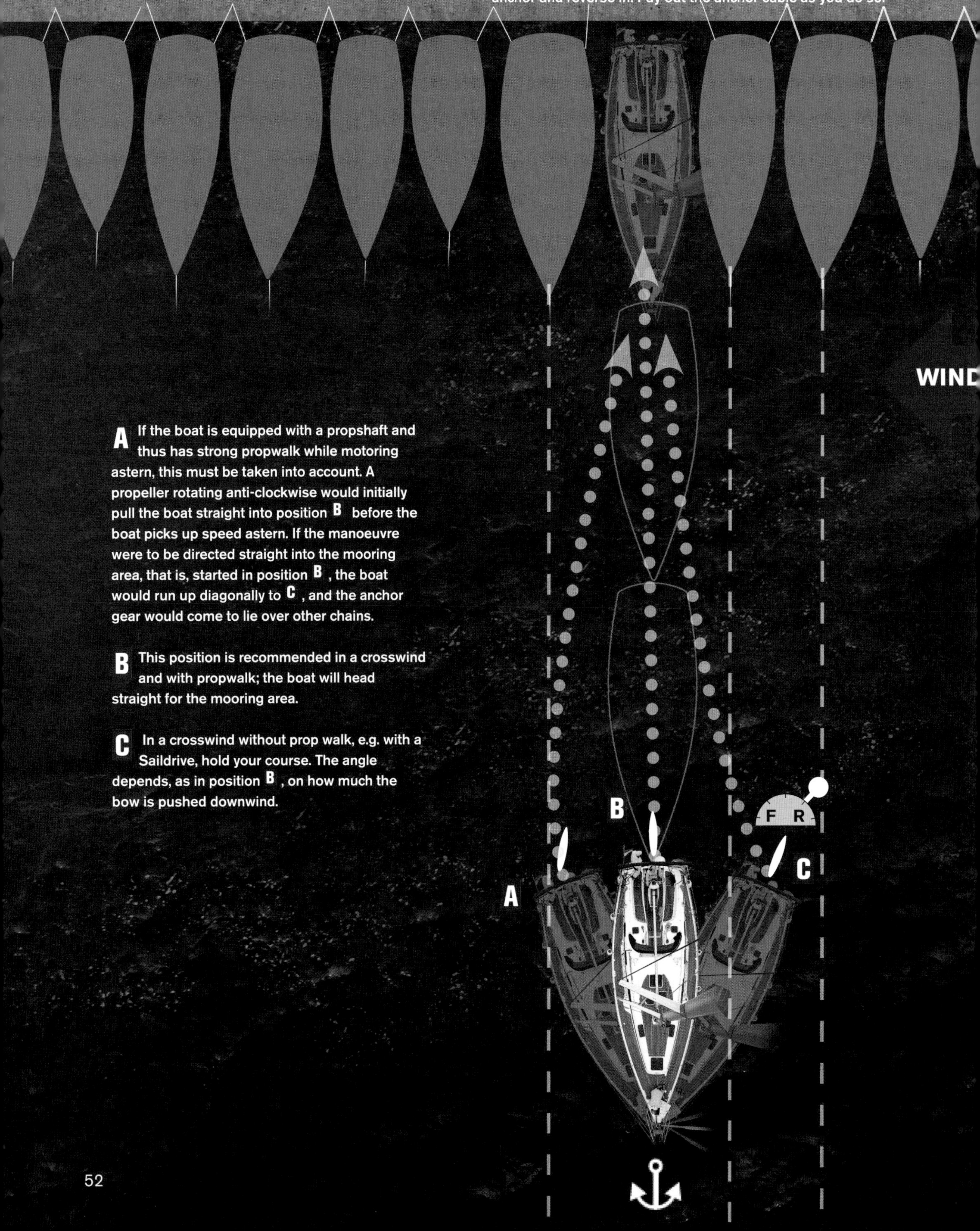

WIND

A If the boat is equipped with a propshaft and thus has strong propwalk while motoring astern, this must be taken into account. A propeller rotating anti-clockwise would initially pull the boat straight into position **B** before the boat picks up speed astern. If the manoeuvre were to be directed straight into the mooring area, that is, started in position **B**, the boat would run up diagonally to **C**, and the anchor gear would come to lie over other chains.

B This position is recommended in a crosswind and with propwalk; the boat will head straight for the mooring area.

C In a crosswind without prop walk, e.g. with a Saildrive, hold your course. The angle depends, as in position **B**, on how much the bow is pushed downwind.

A

B

F R

C

The Mediterranean moor

Anchoring greatly reduces your scope for manoeuvring: there is only a narrow lane available, because your chain shouldn't lie over your neighbour's. In addition the approach begins much earlier so you can pay out the necessary length of chain. Before you begin agree the steps of the manoeuvre with the crew. A good rule of thumb for deciding on the length of chain is five times the depth of the water and at least three times the length of the boat.

When approaching the mooring lower the anchor to the surface of the water. This way it's guaranteed to fall clear. Hand signals should be agreed upon for communication between the bowman and the helmsman. (It's more professional, and safer in noisy surroundings.) So the helmsman's circling forefinger can mean 'keep paying out', a balled fist means 'stop'.

On the helmsman's command the bowman lets the anchor run out quickly till it hits the bottom, then controls the chain by hand with a capstan brake. Paying out by means of an electric drive generally takes too long and in the meantime the boat can drift. During the approach to the mooring the bowman keeps paying out. Then a few metres from the dock the chain is slowed down gently so that the anchor digs in. However, don't bring the boat to a standstill while doing this. As soon as the windward mooring line is secure, motor about at least half a boat's length from the dock and pull the chain taut with the winch so the anchor digs in. Then you can adjust the length of the chain and mooring lines as is appropriate.

The correct position at the wheel

Steering astern with a wheel is a specialized skill. If you stand holding the wheel in the usual way you'll have to rethink what you're doing: left is right and right is left. A remedy for this is to turn round.

OVER THE SHOULDER

An unergonomic way of standing, and in addition you have to mentally re-think which way to turn the wheel. This is often difficult for an inexperienced helmsman.

IN FRONT OF THE WHEEL

A good position for a helmsman who has a problem with sailing backwards. Operating controls and steering are done in the same direction as when motoring forwards.

WITH THE WHEEL BEHIND YOUR BACK

Another practical variation for avoiding mistakes when sailing backwards. But operating the controls is a little difficult!

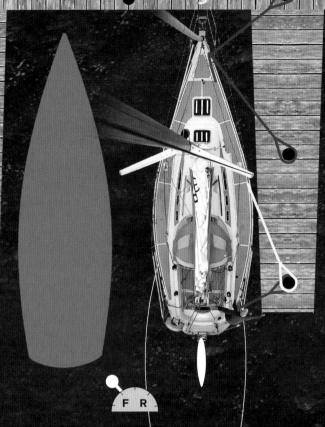
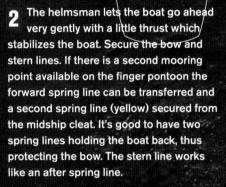
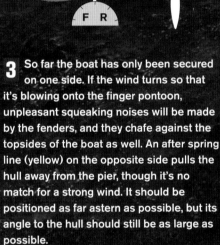

2 The helmsman lets the boat go ahead very gently with a little thrust which stabilizes the boat. Secure the bow and stern lines. If there is a second mooring point available on the finger pontoon the forward spring line can be transferred and a second spring line (yellow) secured from the midship cleat. It's good to have two spring lines holding the boat back, thus protecting the bow. The stern line works like an after spring line.

3 So far the boat has only been secured on one side. If the wind turns so that it's blowing onto the finger pontoon, unpleasant squeaking noises will be made by the fenders, and they chafe against the topsides of the boat as well. An after spring line (yellow) on the opposite side pulls the hull away from the pier, though it's no match for a strong wind. It should be positioned as far astern as possible, but its angle to the hull should still be as large as possible.

Tying up correctly

Finger pontoons are extraordinary! They are mostly used as a floating variation in harbours that are dependent on the tide. This avoids the very complex way of tying up described on page 41. They are most commonly found in British marinas. They make it easier to get on and off the boat over the side of the hull. However, they usually have a disadvantage: they're too short to use a stern line as a brake. Instead you can use the engine to stop, and in addition the forward spring line.

1 The approach is made depending on the direction of the wind (as when tying up at a jetty with mooring posts). It may be necessary to hold back, or to proceed with a little more thrust. Prepare a forward spring line as well as two bow lines and a stern line on the 'shore-side'. As soon as the finger pier is within reach a crew member climbs over the side and belays the forward spring line. For a two-man crew the spring line should then be taken back to the cockpit for adjustment. As soon as the forward spring line is tight, angle the rudder a little away from the pier to get the boat straight.

Using a forward spring line

In tight harbours with narrow lanes, where the sterns of other boats stick out, a direct approach to the mooring area may not be possible since there isn't enough space for turning. Here too the forward spring line is the method of choice, but this time as a manoeuvring line rather than as a mooring line.

2 The crew climbs onto the finger pontoon as soon as it's within reach and belays the forward spring line. The helmsman can now drive gently against this, turning the rudder towards the pier to assist the turn. The side next to the pontoon must be well fendered. When the boat has come parallel to the pier, slowly pay out the forward spring line and tie up as described opposite.

1 Make the approach in the middle of the lane to keep as clear as possible of other boats on either side. A crew member stands level with the spreaders ready with the forward spring line, which with a two-man crew is run back to the helmsman. All other available crew are divided up on each side to fend off. A large spherical fender is useful as the final means of braking.

WIND   **CURRENT**

It's easier to pick up a buoy astern

Mooring buoys are popular with most sailors. They spare you the often laborious rigmarole with your own anchor. But many crews make things unnecessarily difficult: they run up to the buoy forwards, then a crew member on the bow tries to make a forward spring line fast to it. This means the helmsman loses sight of the buoy as soon as it disappears in the blind spot in front of the bow. In addition the wind and the current blow the bow off-course from the buoy. But even when it's right on target, there is often another problem: a modern 10-metre yacht has a freeboard height of at least 1.3 metres at the bow. But the average adult, lying flat on the deck with his arm outstretched, only has a reach of some 70 to 80 centimetres! The eye of the buoy must then be at least 50 centimetres high so that a mooring line can be pushed through it. If it's too low it results in risky contortions or games of dexterity with a boathook.

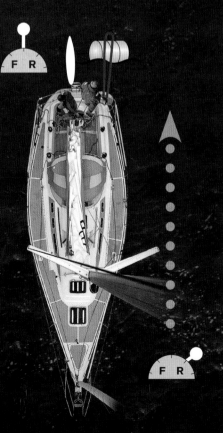

1 Approach the buoy stern first. As you do this be careful to steer accurately against the wind or the current or their combination. That way the boat will stay on course and not swing sideways. About two boat's lengths from the buoy reduce speed to a crawl, because the propeller's slipstream from a sharp forward burst on the motor as you stop would wash the buoy away from the stern. When the buoy is within reach rig a slip rope through the eye. Now the boat is lying secure. If the wind is strong you may have to run the engine gently in astern.

2 Now, at your leisure, you can rig a bow line (yellow), which must be at least two and a half times the length of the boat. Then take this line astern, outboard of everything, run it through the eye of the mooring buoy and bring it back to the bow. Only one person is needed to do this.

3 Pay out the stern line slowly and haul in the bow line at the same speed – over a winch if necessary. This way there will be no danger to neighbouring boats and the turn will be accomplished in a relaxed manner.

4 For the final part of the manoeuvre, when the bow has swung round close to the buoy, then retrieve the stern line. The boat straightens up. Cleat the bow line so it's ready for casting off quickly.

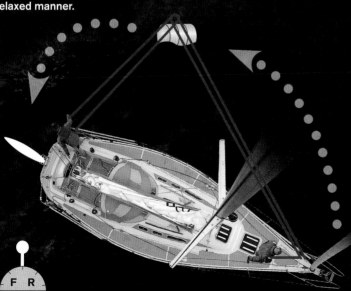

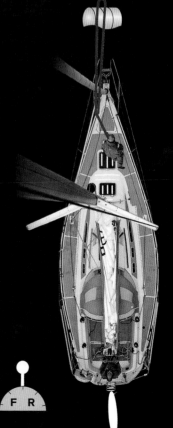

A fine art

Knowing how to tie up without using the motor is a requirement of good seamanship and at the same time one of the most demanding tasks for a skipper and his crew.

There are many arguments against manoeuvring under sail in a harbour – but there's no reason for not knowing how to do it. Of course harbours today are very narrow, boats are very big and motors are very reliable. But there's still that unexpected joker in the pack: he usually appears in a strong wind and high seas, when the residue in the diesel tank has been churned up and blocked the fuel filter. Then there's nothing for it but to fall back on your own abilities.

And these need to be honed. The drills in this chapter can be – and need to be – repeated again and again on days when the wind is light, at an empty pier, a secluded jetty or with a fender lowered to an anchor as a fixed marker. Being able to control the boat without using the engine is a requirement of good seamanship.

Practice is so important because it is vital that, under sail, you can calculate your speed, the remaining distance to be covered and the correct course. Every boat reacts differently depending on her draught, the shape of the hull and the keel as well as her sailing characteristics, so the skipper has first to develop a feel for the boat: how long she takes to stop, how she reacts to the rudder under full sail or with only the mainsail or with only the headsail. It's also necessary to establish the diameter of the turning circle under sail and to make a mental note of it as described in the quick stop on page 141. The turning circle also plays a role in some of the situations on the following pages.

In addition to the actual mooring man-oeuvres, preparation is vital for success. This means studying the handbook carefully before any approach to an unknown harbour,

as well as a strategy to deal with engine failure. So a skipper must know where dangerous situations from onshore winds close to the coast may occur; in addition it's important to avoid sailing into a cul-de-sac. The diagram on page 61 shows the critical area. The strategy also includes sailing on if necessary and making for another harbour, for example a fishing harbour, which can probably offer a longer pier. Another possibility would be to anchor outside the harbour and try to organize help, perhaps by calling for a tow or by using your own dinghy. These can be the safest options in a very crowded harbour – rather than sailing in under wind power.

It goes without saying that berthing under sail carries a significantly greater risk of damage than berthing under power, in particular with a large or heavy boat. There is very little room for error because you can't use a short burst astern from the motor to brake. Therefore the anchor should always be clear and a stern anchor should be lying ready. In particular, make sure the boat is well fendered.

When berthing in such conditions it's not important to reach the ideal mooring place immediately. It's much more impor-tant to tie up at a berth that has room to manoeuvre to leeward. That could be at a mooring post, another boat or a pier. Since berthing manoeuvres under sail are usually hardly ever practised, most people on board are generally much more nervous than under normal circumstances, which means more room for error. So the motto is: establish calm in the boat, get a line ashore, cool down frayed nerves and then think about the next step.

The dinghy as a tug

In calm conditions even a little outboard motor can be a great help, and it can also move relatively big boats. A dinghy tow is better than trying to sail with very little speed.

The dinghy is made fast alongside with bow and stern lines and – very important – a forward spring line. These transfer the forces from the dinghy. The power comes from the outboard motor but the steering is done on the yacht, where lines lie ready forward, amidships and astern on both sides. The stern anchor must also be clear because you can only brake over a very long distance, if at all. Wherever possible use a line for stopping.

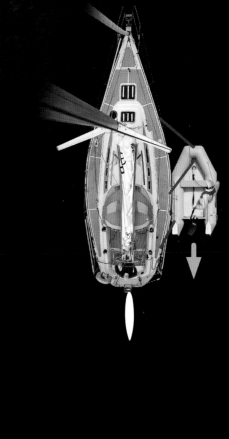

Keep calm and carry on

One of the most important aims when berthing under sail is to
have the boat under control at all times, so we recommend that you
first tie up somewhere to leeward, be it to a mooring post, a jetty, a
pier or another boat. As soon as a bow line has been secured the
boat is safe, the sail area can be reduced, things will become
clearer and further action can be discussed calmly. A crew member
can often now be sent ashore to help at the final mooring place. Or
the motor can be quietly repaired *in situ*!

WIND

Securing room to manoeuvre

In this example of a small harbour the areas marked in red should be avoided during the first approach if the crew don't know the locality. This way the skipper can avoid getting into a lee shore situation or a row of berths that is in fact a cul-de-sac which is too narrow to turn in. Instead, go for the safer areas to the right of the diagram.

U-Stop

This manoeuvre is particularly suitable for bringing modern short keelers (which have a tight turning circle) to a stop, for instance when running up to a buoy or at the start of an anchoring manoeuvre. The headsail should first be taken in so that the surface area doesn't act as a brake and to make enough room to work on the foredeck.

1 The helmsman chooses a course which, depending on its turning circle, will bring the boat to within one to one and a half boat lengths of the buoy or the desired anchoring place. When this point is roughly abeam of the helmsman he puts the rudder hard over.

2 The mainsail isn't used, it's allowed to flutter. The boat executes a sharp turn during which she turns head to wind. Usually she ends up stopping in exactly the right place.

3 Now the bowman can hook the buoy or drop the anchor. The quick-stop should be practised frequently, using an improvised buoy in open water.

Skilfully into the wind

The most important features of anchoring under sail are the three kinds of stopping by sailing into the wind: the U-stop, sailing almost head-to-wind and sailing totally head-to-wind. They crop up again and again in various forms and should therefore be practised at regular intervals to refresh the memory and definitely by charter skippers before beginning a cruise – as should the man overboard procedure. It takes about half an hour, and a life jacket or a fender can be used as a buoy. You should also practise backing the headsail and mainsail for braking manoeuvres.

Almost head-to-wind

This differs from being totally head-to-wind in the approach angle. The starting point is a beam reach about two or three boat lengths to leeward of the stopping point, here a buoy. The actual distance depends on the boat. With heavy boats or in high seas a longer approach will be necessary; dinghies stop almost immediately when they go head-to-wind.

2 Cast off the sheets, allowing the sails to flap. Let the boat drift to the buoy; if there's a danger of her not reaching it, carefully pick up a little speed using the mainsail. The advantage of this approach is that both course and speed can be corrected right up to the end.

45°

Totally head-to-wind

Going totally head-to-wind is an all-or-nothing manoeuvre. If the boat is going too slowly it will 'starve to death' before it reaches the point it's aiming for and start to drift – this can be dangerous in a harbour.

However, the reverse isn't much better: if the boat has too much momentum it'll overshoot the buoy, with similar risks. It's even more important to practise this manoeuvre than it is the other two variations because this one has to be done time and again. This is the only possible way to make way against the wind without a motor – only a few metres, but enough to reach a berth in one go in an offshore wind.

1 If the boat is easily manoeuvrable with the mainsail, take in the headsail to give more room on the foredeck. The helmsman turns 45 degrees towards the buoy from a point about two to three boat lengths to leeward of the buoy (broken line on the right).

1 Choosing the right moment here is vital. Depending on the turning circle of the boat, start the manoeuvre by bringing the rudder hard over so that the bow is then pointing straight at the buoy, directly into the wind. The sails don't do anything here except flap.

63

3 The bowman hands over a bow line to a helper or jumps ashore himself. Quickly secure the bow line before the boat begins to drift. You'll have plenty of time for all the other lines once the boat has been secured.

Head-to-wind into the berth

Sailing completely head-to-wind is the only way possible of reaching this berth in one go against the wind. When it's not blowing too hard there's no problem. The boat can be gently slowed down with a line. If the turn doesn't reach, you can easily work your way hand-over-hand alongside the neighbouring boat or use the method on the opposite pages. This would also be recommended in a strong wind.

2b Instead of the stern line, or in addition to it, a midship spring line (or a forward spring line) is secured. If there are enough crew members on board then both can be attached. This has the advantage that, if the boat doesn't have enough momentum or if the berth is very short, the stopping distance is increased. But be careful: if you only use one midship spring line this pulls the boat right off course as she stops.

1 Sail the boat up to the line of mooring posts with enough speed. If there's enough wind blowing take in the headsail early, or at the very latest when starting to sail head-to-wind. This makes room on the foredeck, and in addition the bow turns more easily to windward.

2a The bowman secures a stern line over one of the berth's two mooring posts. In a short berth he should do this from a position as far forward as possible on the deck so he is forward, ready with the bow line. This line is more important than the stern lines, which can be secured later. The helmsman or another crew member takes in the slack on the stern line and uses it to slow the boat down, which works very well in a long berth. In short berths midship spring lines, as in the example on the right, can be better.

3 Use muscle power to pull the boat to the jetty and secure the bow line to a bollard, ring or cleat. This method may not work with heavier boats, in which case the boat can be moved with the aft spring line using a winch, while the person on shore just takes in the slack on the bow line and uses it to control the direction. The aft spring line can then be used as a mooring line. However, moving the boat with an aft spring pulls her forward only until the stern reaches the post. Alternatively, the bow line can also be left belayed on shore, and it can then be hauled in by the combined efforts of those remaining on board or by using a winch.

2 Secure a bow line to a post. The boat is now secured, and the sail can be taken in. Now take a long bow line to shore over a neighbouring boat. If that's not possible and the distance is too great to throw a line use the dinghy. Or a helper can 'float' a line attached to a fender from the shore down to the yacht.

1 The approach is carried out diagonally and almost head-to-wind. If the helmsman misses the mooring post he was aiming for, the next one within reach can easily be used. The boat can be hauled in afterwards. Be careful if the sterns of other boats are protruding into the lane.

More control

A somewhat safer method when it's windier or when the crew isn't experienced is to tie up outside the berth and haul the boat in manually. It's also suitable if you overshoot the first mooring post at the first approach. In addition the manoeuvre can be aborted at any time by falling off, which isn't possible with the variation on the left once the bow is between the mooring posts.

1a The classic method is to ease your way into the berth using the anchor. If there's enough space the stern anchor is dropped and you pay out chain to ease the boat into the berth with the least amount of sail or even using the boat's windage. Dig in the anchor and stop in good time. You can also begin by sailing head-to-wind and using the bow anchor. After tying up, the anchor can be brought in by the dinghy or it can remain while you're lying in harbour. In that case the chain should be paid out as far as the bottom so that it doesn't become an obstacle for others.

With wind power

An onshore wind is actually the best scenario for getting to a mooring to leeward. Practically nothing can go wrong when the wind works as propulsion – except you can't turn it off! The most important thing in any of the actions is to be able to stop the boat safely, otherwise she – and most probably other boats – will sustain damage.

1b In very light winds you can proceed without dropping anchor, but there can also be other reasons for not doing so, such as an unstable anchor ground, not enough room to anchor or a ban on anchoring. Then you have to sail straight into the berth. To do this reduce speed to just enough for manoeuvring by reducing the sail area, and if need be sail the boat head-to-wind.

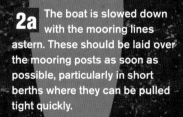

2a The boat is slowed down with the mooring lines astern. These should be laid over the mooring posts as soon as possible, particularly in short berths where they can be pulled tight quickly.

2b In a short berth it can be safer to replace at least one, or if enough hands are available both, of the after mooring lines with a midship or forward spring line. Though these also pull the boat off-course, they do extend the stopping distance if required.

1a A very safe approach path for this manoeuvre is on the windward side of the mooring lane, under the headsail alone (under no circumstances leave the mainsail set). As soon as you can see a space on the leeward side put a slipped stern line over the mooring post opposite and bring the boat to a controlled stop by carefully paying out the line. At the same time, or at the very latest when the boat has stopped, take in the rest of the sails. Now you can secure a bow line as well if you want and haul the boat sideways. Once you're in position, let the wind push the bow downwind (if the mainsail was still set, this could be unpleasant). The stern line remains belayed for the time being.

1b You can steer towards your chosen mooring post by going head-to-wind, for instance when the mainsail is set. It's best here to have the sail quietly taken in as soon as the boat is secured to the mooring post. The bow line must be set as a slip line. After that, secure a slip stern line. Slowly pay out the bow line, in a very narrow lane hauling in the stern line with a winch at the same time. The boat will turn. Now retrieve the bow line.

With the brake

In modern marinas with mooring lanes a mooring post can take over the function of an anchor. In fact it often has to do this when the lanes are too tight for turning head-to-wind or for any kind of manoeuvre with sails. Even if you're tempted to sail straight into a mooring space on the leeward side it's a good idea to secure the boat first and to think it over in peace and quiet. Because if the approach with a tight turn doesn't work, the boat will end up against the mooring posts on a lee shore.

2 If the boat turns round so far that she's lying opposite the berth, pay out the stern line until a second stern line can be secured over one of the mooring posts at the berth. Make the boat secure and haul in the long stern line.

Sailing straight in

Manoeuvring into a berth under sail is tempting in a crosswind. But don't underestimate the risks. Sailing into the berth head-to-wind isn't applicable and you can only slow down by means of a line. In addition there is also a real danger of hooking a sail or a sheet onto a mooring post or a nearby boat. The result would be chaos. Correctly practised, though, mooring on a beam reach, at least when the wind isn't blowing strongly, counts as a safe manoeuvre.

2 Brake using a forward or midship spring line, which extends the distance for braking, and secure the boat to windward. Quickly secure a bow line on the windward side and a mooring line astern on the windward side. There is plenty of time for setting the leeward lines.

1 Reduce the sail area to the absolute minimum, depending on the strength of the wind. Take in the mainsail completely (otherwise the boom may get caught or may hit a nearby boat, and you won't be able to let out the mainsail far enough to stop). Have forward and/or midship spring lines ready, also a stern line and a bow line.

Gentle braking

This before-the-wind manoeuvre can be helpful when there's only limited room to manoeuvre in the lane.

A Slow the boat down using a slip stern line. You don't need other securing lines at this stage. If the mooring area is ahead, the boat can be turned into the berth as described on page 69.

B If you overshoot the mooring you could turn the boat and berth her as described on the right.

With the aid of a line

Whichever approach situation you start with, the finale of this manoeuvre is the same: lines are used to pull the boat into the mooring area in a controlled, measured and safe way. Many of the disadvantages mentioned on the left-hand page disappear when sailing straight in.

2 Rig an aft spring line in addition to the bow line. Using these and the winch, move the boat forward to the windward mooring post. Secure a bow line to the next boat or as described on page 65. Pull the boat into the berth by means of the bow line, which can be assisted by hauling the aft spring line. If a worry line (blue, dotted) is available use it to secure the bow against drifting. Secure a windward stern line in good time. The aft spring line now becomes the leeward stern line.

WIND

1b Going totally head-to-wind is only an option if there's plenty of room to manoeuvre outside the row of mooring posts. This is a good way to slow down, which is why the head-to-wind alternative is recommended for nervous skippers. It also makes life easier because there aren't any obstacles ahead so it doesn't matter whether the stopping distance has been calculated correctly. Just before the boat stops she's secured to the next mooring post within reach with a bow line and the sails are taken in. Once she's reached the leeward or windward mooring post of the berth you want, proceed further as described, otherwise move her there with the aid of a line.

1a When the wind is astern you shouldn't steer into a mooring lane with the mainsail unless you know there's enough room to turn. With the headsail set the 180-degree turn into the wind is a safe way of stopping the boat. It's important with this variation that the headsail is fully eased or handed as soon as the wind comes abeam into it – otherwise the turning of the bow against the wind is slowed down by this surface. At the end of the manoeuvre secure a bow line over the best mooring post, take in the sails and continue as described above.

WIND

2b At the first opportunity a crew member goes on shore with a line or hands it to a helper. If there's enough space available you can use the stern line to brake (right). But if there isn't enough space then using a midship spring line extends the distance available for braking. The helmsman brings the boat alongside and braking is achieved with the midship line over a bollard. Then secure the bow and stern lines.

2c If stopping at the mooring area is too risky you can also come alongside another boat first. Then the boat is hauled in hand over hand with the aid of a line.

Bow first

2a In a short mooring area it's enough to bring the boat as close to land as possible and initially secure a bow line. Then you can take in the sail in peace and quiet, and finally haul the boat in hand over hand with the aid of a stern line.

With an offshore wind there are several alternative methods of berthing under sail. Here, too, avoid going totally head-to-wind. If you fall short a new approach can usually be started, but if you're going too fast a crash becomes almost inevitable because there's no possibility of braking except with the stern anchor. (And even this possibility is rather theoretical since from the moment the crew notices there's a problem to the fall and digging in of the anchor so much time passes that you really don't have a chance to stop. On the other hand the approach almost head-to-wind is far safer. The manoeuvres are shown here with the headsail. You can also sail in with the mainsail, only then there's the danger that you won't be able to reduce your speed by letting out the mainsail, especially if the boat has angled spreaders.

1a Approaching with a tack gives you a good chance of slowing the boat down. When the speed drops after the tack the correct angle for the approach can be estimated reasonably accurately.

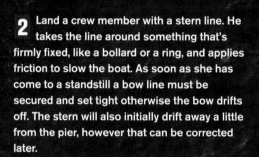

2 Land a crew member with a stern line. He takes the line around something that's firmly fixed, like a bollard or a ring, and applies friction to slow the boat. As soon as she has come to a standstill a bow line must be secured and set tight otherwise the bow drifts off. The stern will also initially drift away a little from the pier, however that can be corrected later.

1 Reduce the sail area to a minimum and decrease speed so that the boat just remains manoeuvrable. Bring the boat alongside the jetty.

Parallel to the dock

If there is enough space available at the dock this is the easiest way of berthing. The speed can be adjusted by trimming the sails. And if you're unsuccessful on the first approach you can easily sail away from the dock for a new attempt.

1b An approach almost head-to-wind is the safest method. By taking bearings forward the drift, or displacement by the current, can be accurately determined and the point you're aiming for targeted reasonably accurately. Moreover, the speed can be adjusted constantly by trimming the sail.

WIND

1 Reduce the sail area to the absolute minimum. The boat is brought up to the jetty, a crew member climbs ashore with a long stern line and slows the boat with it over a bollard or a cleat on the jetty.

With a stern line

The prerequisite for this manoeuvre is a long empty pier, because it's difficult to estimate the braking distance and the danger of colliding with another boat is high. All the more so in a high wind, when even running under a bare mast generates considerable forward speed. Therefore definitely have the stern anchor ready and drop it at the first sign that the manoeuvre is not going to work and cannot be corrected.

2 Immediately after sending the brakeman ashore all the canvas should be taken in. Fender well, especially astern. Once the boat is attached safely by the stern line all the other lines can be secured.

Head-to-wind

In this example it's clear why it's so important to master different aspects of sailing into the wind.

1a The 180-degree turn into the wind begins directly opposite the mooring you're aiming for, since this usually lets you reach it safely. The only risk is when the distance to the jetty at the start of the manoeuvre is too short – then a collision is bound to happen since by the time the helmsman notices the mistake it's too late to get out of the way. Anyone who is uncertain would do better to leave too much transverse distance; you can always steer a little more towards the dock before the boat come to rest.

2 Lower all available fenders on the shore side. A bow line must be secured as soon as possible. Once this has been done the boat is attached safely. The skipper can decide whether to take in the sail first or to secure more lines.

1b Here we are sailing close-hauled, having come from the downwind course via a beam reach. The boat is well under control from adjusting the mainsail as she makes for the mooring. Since both course and speed are easy to adjust you can run into a tighter space at a jetty. And if the helmsman still misjudges it, he can quite easily defuse a dangerous situation with a totally head-to-wind manoeuvre and, if necessary, tack away.

1c Here it's clear why a totally head-to-wind course is known as an all-or-nothing manoeuvre. If the helmsman misjudges it, the boat crashes. It either collides with the jetty or with a boat tied up to windward. In addition a large space at the jetty is needed, depending on the boat's approach. Therefore the almost head-to-wind course is preferred.

73

WIND

1 Sail totally head-to-wind for a sufficient distance. As soon as the boat comes to a standstill, drop anchor. If later on the anchor is to be hauled in from the dinghy, at all costs make fast a tripping line or a buoy first. Take in the sails.

2 Pay out the anchor cable until the boat is lying with her stern just off the jetty. It's not important for the anchor to dig in completely, it's only being used to slow the boat down.

With an anchor

An onshore wind is supposedly the best direction for berthing under sail. After all, the wind takes over the role of propulsion to the mooring area. In light conditions, therefore, just allow yourself to be carried to the mooring and lower fenders to protect against sailing into the jetty. But always take in the sails first. Otherwise you may be pushed onto the jetty, which can result in heeling, acceleration and chaos. This method isn't suitable in a stronger wind. Then the boat can drift so much or continue to pick up so much speed that damage is sustained either to her or to other boats. So an anchoring method, such as a Mediterranean moor and then hauling the boat in, is a safer alternative.

3 Secure a stern line, put all available fenders over the side near the stern, then pay out the anchor cable so the boat turns to the jetty. Finally tie up. Lastly, retrieve the anchor from the dinghy.

1 Sail into the wind at a safe distance from the pier. Drop the mainsail now, if you haven't done this earlier.

Swinging in

If you can't drop anchor, this method is another way of reducing excess speed. However, you need to be well in control of the boat first and it's not as precise as anchoring.

2 Fall away with just the headsail, with its area reduced to the point where the boat remains just manoeuvrable. Lower as many fenders as possible to leeward.

3 Just before you reach the jetty luff hard, then immediately bear away until the boat is lying almost parallel to the jetty. Take in the rest of the headsail or let it flap. The bow should still point a little to windward, because it blows downwind the fastest. The boat should now be almost stationary and will slowly drift onto the jetty. A stern line should be secured first to bring the boat to a standstill in case she picks up speed again.

1 Sail totally head-to-wind for a sufficient distance. As soon as the boat comes to a standstill, drop anchor. A sail can remain set to help the anchor dig in.

2 Back the headsail or the mainsail and pay out the anchor cable with resistance so that the anchor digs in. Take the sail in just before the pier and let the boat drift to the mooring.

Mediterranean moor

The classic method of berthing in the Mediterranean Sea only works under sail in an onshore wind. Then the normal anchor manoeuvre can be carried out.

3 Two to three metres from the pier make the anchor cable fast. Secure stern lines. Lay the stern lines over a winch and slowly winch the boat in close. That way it will be under control, whether the anchor is holding or whether it needs to dig in a little more. The stern lines can stay attached.

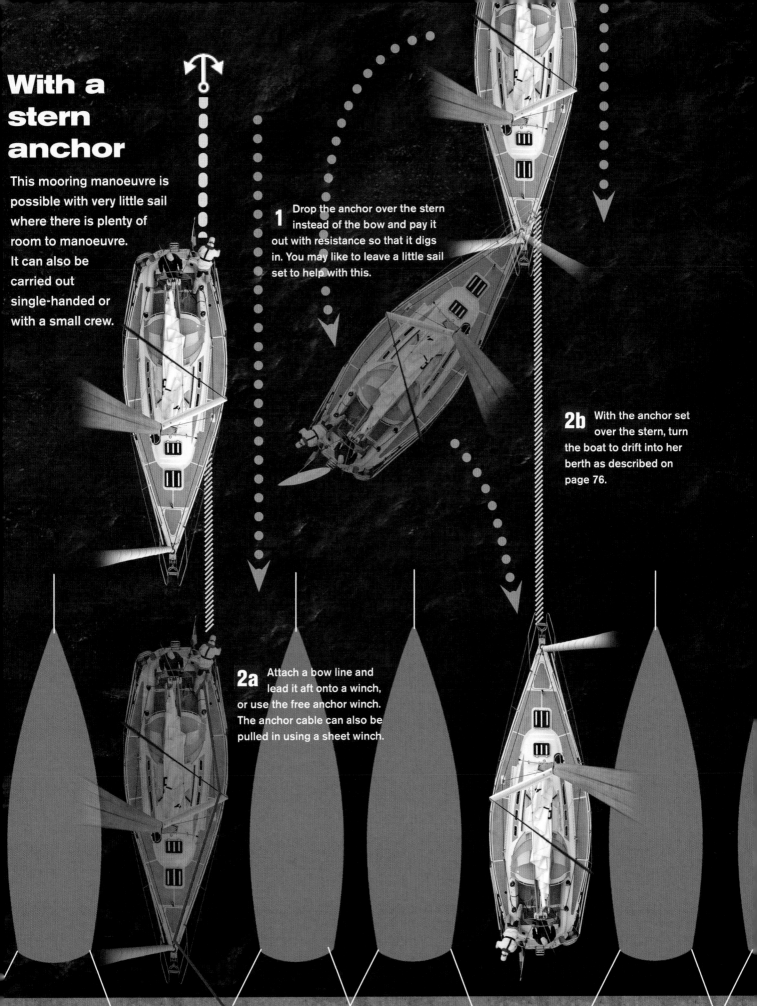

With a stern anchor

This mooring manoeuvre is possible with very little sail where there is plenty of room to manoeuvre. It can also be carried out single-handed or with a small crew.

1 Drop the anchor over the stern instead of the bow and pay it out with resistance so that it digs in. You may like to leave a little sail set to help with this.

2b With the anchor set over the stern, turn the boat to drift into her berth as described on page 76.

2a Attach a bow line and lead it aft onto a winch, or use the free anchor winch. The anchor cable can also be pulled in using a sheet winch.

WIND

3 Fasten the manoeuvring line to the stern. Once the boat is made fast with mooring lines the anchor can be hauled up, otherwise the anchor cable can be hauled in when you haul in the line. In a moderate wind the line can be hauled in hand over hand, or with the help of a winch. Make fast as already described.

In a roundabout way

Whereas you can still sail directly and at a slow speed into a berth when the wind is parallel to the pier, as described on page 27, the alternatives are rather modest in an offshore wind. Unlike berthing parallel to the pier you can't sail directly up to it since other boats are blocking the way. All that remains is the risky totally head-to-wind course (page 63) or the other boats can be used as mooring posts. Leaving aside the great delight of the other owners at this prospect, this isn't exactly easy because of the mooring line and the anchor tackle. These frequently prevent you from getting within range of another boat. Then another manoeuvring line is needed, assuming there isn't, as with the other manoeuvres, a helper with a rubber dinghy with a motor which can tow the boat to the mooring area.

2 With your own dinghy secure a shore line, or perhaps a helper will offer to do this. An alternative is to send out the line to the boat on a fender or some other large floating object.

1 If you've tied up with mooring lines the anchor should be dropped as close as possible to the other boats. That saves making a trip later. With the help of the angles of the other mooring lines you can estimate roughly where the bottom weights lie. In that case the anchor can remain up and down, it only has to hold temporarily. If you tie up with a Mediterranean moor drop the anchor in the optimal position, that is, where you would also do it with the help of a motor. Here too at this stage it can remain up and down.

3 When there is very little wind you can now work your way along the other boats to the pier. Otherwise take a second mooring line astern to the pier and haul the boat in the last little bit over the winch.

1 Under no circumstances should you make your approach with the mainsail set, this will only get in the way of falling away later. Steer as close as you can to your future neighbour using just the little bit of speed remaining. Transfer a long line; a well-aimed throw is helpful here.

2 Fall away and at the same time hand the rest of the sails. The helper should now have made the line fast. Just before this becomes taut drop a little of it overboard over a winch so that the line doesn't move. That also protects the helper's boat. Now winch in to the other boat.

Risky

Anyone who wants to cut out the anchor or using a dinghy can also try this way of getting a line to shore. This works very well at a mooring, particularly if its lines slope down into the water. If the other boats are lying on a bow anchor and the harbour is shallow you shouldn't risk this manoeuvre, otherwise the keel or the rudder will get caught and if another boat's anchor breaks out as a result there will be great howls of protest. This manoeuvre only works anyway if the boat you're going to tie up next to helps or a crew member has been set ashore somewhere else in the harbour and has boarded that boat. Ask first!

WIND

A Approach the mooring area by going head-to-wind: this works quite well if the berth isn't too narrow, in which case there's not enough room to turn. The important thing is to secure the forward spring line quickly. As the boat slows down the bow turns towards the finger pier and the stern towards the next boat. So always make sure there are plenty of fenders lowered. If the midship spring line is secured at the same time as the forward spring line the angular momentum can be reduced.

B If the lane is too narrow to turn straight into the berth a crew member can also be put down on the head of the pier to pull the boat into the berth in your own time. This variation is also recommended for all those who are unsure of or unpractised in the manoeuvre.

C It's actually easier to berth before the wind than with mooring posts since the boat can be slowed down along the whole of the jetty. Nevertheless, hauling on a stern line offers even more control, particularly when it's very windy or the current is strong.

With a forward spring line and foresight

The specific features of berthing in harbour at a finger pier come into their own even more when berthing under sail. The sterns protruding into the lane are a phalanx of obstacles. But the jetties also have an advantage: the distance available for slowing down is extended enormously since a crew member can be set down on the pier well before you reach your actual jetty. In addition you can leave out the moving with the aid of a line already described because the way between a 'mooring post', that is the end of the finger pier, and the jetty is accessible. Otherwise the same techniques are just as applicable to jetties with mooring posts. With one exception: you can't use a stern line to slow a boat down if, as usually happens, your own boat is longer than the finger pier. Therefore the forward spring line takes on a particular importance. A midship spring line shouldn't be used, since many finger piers are so short that only a short braking distance is available.

D Also with a beam reach or coming from a course before the wind there are hardly any differences from berthing at a mooring post, except that once again you use the forward spring line to slow down instead of the stern line, and that the unprotected sterns of the other boats must be given particular attention.

WIND

1 The skipper selects a position on the wrong side of the lane so that he has as much room to turn as possible. Take particular care to look out for other boats when doing this. Rudder hard to starboard and a forward burst on the motor starts the turn.

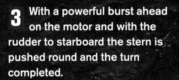

2 Give a powerful burst astern on the motor. If the lane is very narrow as here the rudder can remain turned to starboard. The travel astern isn't long enough to pick up appreciable speed for any noticeable effect of the rudder being astern. Prop walk pulls the stern to leeward. This effect is still assisted through the starboard rudder, since the stern can slip to port with little resistance.

3 With a powerful burst ahead on the motor and with the rudder to starboard the stern is pushed round and the turn completed.

Turning quickly or lane tango

There are various reasons for turning round in a berthing lane. For example, if you can't find a free space to tie up in and have to leave the lane. If you've entered the lane with the wind astern it's often best to simply leave by motoring backwards, at least if the boat can be easily steered backwards, as is the case with short keelers. But if there is a space to tie up in, it's easier to steer into it against the wind rather than with a following wind. Otherwise the effects described on pages 30 and 32 can occur. But in that case you have to turn round. Depending on the engine system, however, there is something important to take into consideration: which way to turn. Both examples deal with a marine shaft device which produces noticeable prop walk with the commonly occurring clockwise propeller when moving ahead. The turn in the example on the left starts in the correct direction, prop walk assists the turn and it succeeds without a problem. However, on the right the direction is anti-clockwise and against the prop walk. That leads to what is known as a 'mooring lane tango'. Boats with a Saildrive which have only weakly developed prop walk should start the turn from the starboard side of the lane according to the rights of way.

1 The skipper stays by the starboard mooring posts, which is correct for the right of way rules. The turn begins with short, sharp bursts on the motor and the rudder hard to port.

2 Stop with a sharp burst astern on the motor just before the port row of mooring posts. Already when stopping, the prop walk of the backwards anti-clockwise propeller pulls the stern to port, that is in the wrong direction and so works against the turn.

3 Stop again in front of the starboard row of mooring posts. With a forward burst on the motor the rudder is hard against the current and pulls the stern round to starboard in the same direction as the forward clockwise rotating propeller. However, the wind will try to push the bows away to starboard, reducing the overall turn. Finally the boat has turned just a little further than after it had first stopped.

4 This forwards movement can continue now until either the turn succeeds bit by bit or the pier at the end of the lane is reached and the boat is lying on a lee shore. It would have been better to make fast immediately at a port-side mooring post briefly at the first stop and to leave the turning up to the wind, as described on page 84.

WIND

1 There needs to be plenty of room at the pier for this manoeuvre. When mooring normally secure an additional short bow line. In an offshore wind an additional long stern line is placed out around the boat as a spring line. Finally let go of all other mooring lines.

2 In an offshore wind and all directions between offshore and parallel the boat now swings away from the pier by itself and finally remains hanging on the bow line in the direction of the wind. In a wind that blows parallel the stern must be pushed off a little.

With the help of the wind

Sometimes it's necessary to turn a boat towards the pier. If, for instance, the wind is dropping and the bow needs to be turned into the wind or you're sailing away under sail against the wind. Or if work on the outer side of the boat needs to be carried out. Then if no motor can be used because it's not available or not working the turn can be carried out by using lines. The wind helps with this, but it must be blowing offshore or parallel to the pier.

3 When the wind is parallel the boat swings round to the pier and only has to be tied up. For all other wind directions up to offshore the boat must be hauled the rest of the way with the stern line already secured.

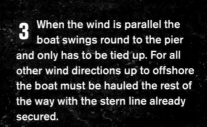

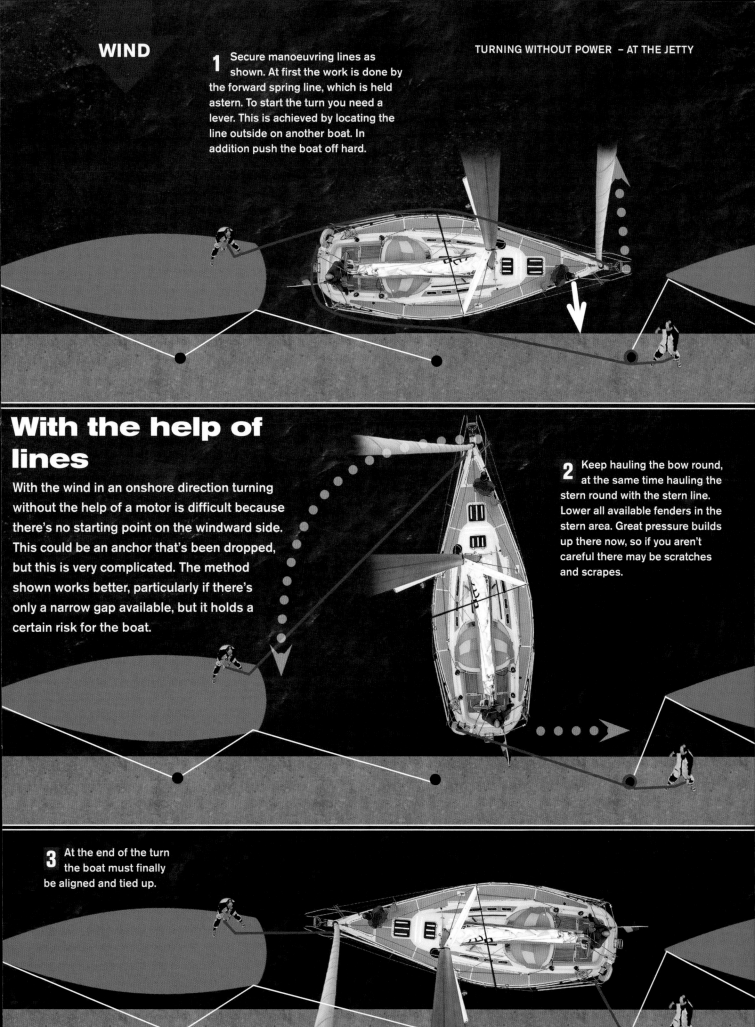

WIND

1 Secure manoeuvring lines as shown. At first the work is done by the forward spring line, which is held astern. To start the turn you need a lever. This is achieved by locating the line outside on another boat. In addition push the boat off hard.

With the help of lines

With the wind in an onshore direction turning without the help of a motor is difficult because there's no starting point on the windward side. This could be an anchor that's been dropped, but this is very complicated. The method shown works better, particularly if there's only a narrow gap available, but it holds a certain risk for the boat.

2 Keep hauling the bow round, at the same time hauling the stern round with the stern line. Lower all available fenders in the stern area. Great pressure builds up there now, so if you aren't careful there may be scratches and scrapes.

3 At the end of the turn the boat must finally be aligned and tied up.

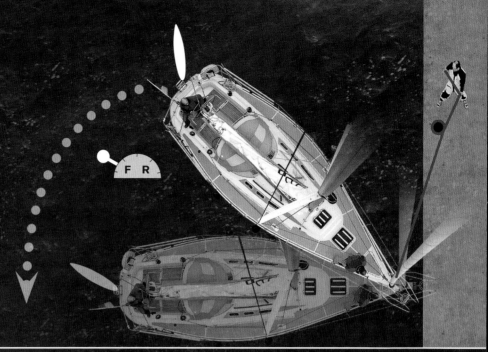

1 Secure a forward spring line, let go all other lines. Lay the rudder towards the land, here hard to port. Slowly increase the thrust ahead, thus easing against the forward spring line, until the stern begins to turn away from the land. The strength of the bursts from the motor determines the speed of the turn.

WIND

With motor power
This is the classic method of turning a boat at a pier with the assistance of a motor, when the wind is blowing more onshore than parallel. Otherwise you can also turn back to the method on page 82. The advantage here over sailing away and then berthing again is that the connection to shore already made doesn't have to be abandoned, which means an increase in safety.

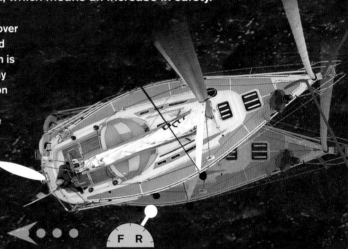

2 As many fenders as possible must be lowered over the bow, since the further the boat swings round the greater the pressure against the pier. If the stern is standing into the wind, the boat can be pushed away from the pier temporarily with a short burst astern on the motor. A propeller which turns clockwise would now assist the turn whilst one turning anticlockwise would work against it. The forward spring line, now the bow line, is hauled in by the person on shore or over a winch on board. Thus the boat lies back again at the starting position. At the same time lower a new forward spring line in the opposite direction to the old one.

3 Step 2 may even be unnecessary; it serves primarily to relieve the bow area. Once the new spring line has been secured you can ease against it again. While you're doing this, pay out the spring line bit by bit until the boat is again lying in its original place.

In a corner

The method is in principle the same as on page 85, except that here a fixed point on the windward side in the form of a pier is available. This kind of turn is helpful, for example, when sailing away under sail in an onshore wind. The turn succeeds very easily but fenders must be lowered as a precaution. There's hardly any friction between the hull and the pier.

1 Secure a long forward spring line to the other side of the pier, and at the same time secure an after spring line to the end of the pier and a stern line to the new pier. These two lines can be operated from on board, one person is enough for that.

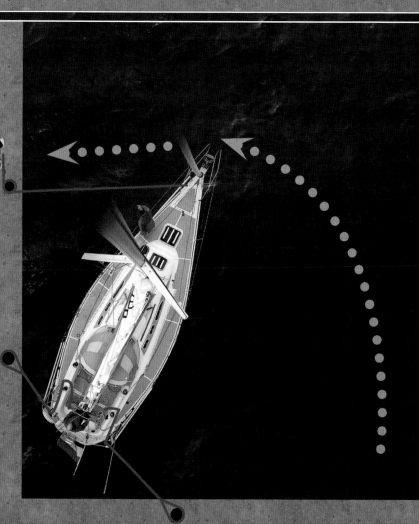

2 With a combined effort the bow is now hauled toward the new pier, thereby pulling through the stern line a little so that the boat pushes off from the original pier. Also take in the stern line a little to assist the turn and push off the stern of the boat from the new pier. If you don't have enough helpers available to pull the bow round or if they can't manage it against the pressure of the wind the line can also be laid over a winch on board towards the stern and hauled in from there.

WIND

Pushing instead of pulling

Should a boat have to be moved to another berth without the use of the motor – because you want to sail away under sail or the distance is only short and the boats lying nearby shouldn't be annoyed by the use of a motor – using lines to assist you is again the obvious thing to do. Often a boat is then pulled as though it's being towed, which however isn't usually the best solution. Three variations for hauling a boat to another pier are shown here.

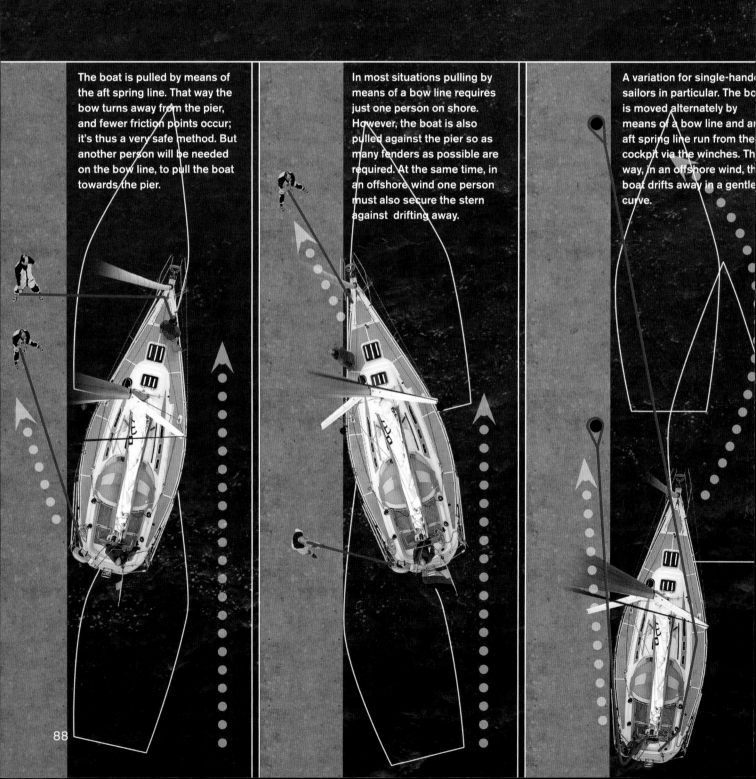

The boat is pulled by means of the aft spring line. That way the bow turns away from the pier, and fewer friction points occur; it's thus a very safe method. But another person will be needed on the bow line, to pull the boat towards the pier.

In most situations pulling by means of a bow line requires just one person on shore. However, the boat is also pulled against the pier so as many fenders as possible are required. At the same time, in an offshore wind one person must also secure the stern against drifting away.

A variation for single-hand sailors in particular. The bo is moved alternately by means of a bow line and a aft spring line run from the cockpit via the winches. Th way, in an offshore wind, th boat drifts away in a gentle curve.

Working your way along

It can also be necessary to move the boat in anchoring places with mooring posts. Just as at the end of a mooring lane, perhaps you want to sail away from there under sail or possibly a berth is available next to friends a couple of metres further on and the skipper doesn't want to risk a completely new run in, possibly when it's too windy.

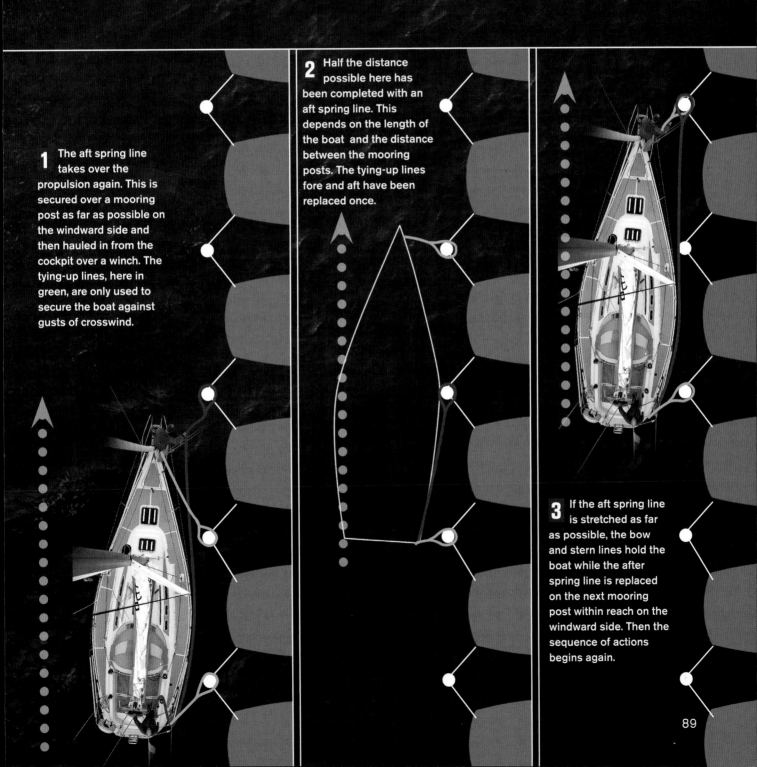

1 The aft spring line takes over the propulsion again. This is secured over a mooring post as far as possible on the windward side and then hauled in from the cockpit over a winch. The tying-up lines, here in green, are only used to secure the boat against gusts of crosswind.

2 Half the distance possible here has been completed with an aft spring line. This depends on the length of the boat and the distance between the mooring posts. The tying-up lines fore and aft have been replaced once.

3 If the aft spring line is stretched as far as possible, the bow and stern lines hold the boat while the after spring line is replaced on the next mooring post within reach on the windward side. Then the sequence of actions begins again.

WIND

1 Secure the bow with a long bow line and haul in both the previous bow lines. If you can find a helper he can pay out the line later and cast off, otherwise for a single-handed sailor loop the bow line back into the cockpit. Pay out the bow line until the stern is positioned between the mooring posts. Haul in the stern line.

2 Pay more of the bow line out slowly, until about two-thirds of the boat has passed the mooring posts. Now haul in the bow line very quickly and move the boat astern in the desired direction with a short burst on the motor and by changing the position of the rudder. Even if the bow line now has a kink in it and is caught you can still secure the boat with another bow line to the mooring post and clear the looped bow line or abort the manoeuvre and move the boat forward under power to start all over again. Should the bow start to drift when hauling in the bow line it doesn't matter since it will be brought to a stop by the mooring post. Then it must be pushed off from the pulpit.

Turning with wind power

To motor away from a berth in an offshore wind counts as one of the easiest manoeuvres of all. That is, when the wind is light. Haul in the bow lines, pull the boat astern using the stern lines, and as soon as the mooring posts are within reach haul in the stern line and leave the berth backwards at a slow speed. However, in a strong wind even this manoeuvre can cause problems if the bow begins to drift off course. That'll please the neighbours! A strong burst astern on the motor will help to counteract this. But this also carries the risk of going too far to leeward – and thus onto the next row of mooring posts. And if a mooring line doesn't come free the boat ends up out of control. Therefore the bow should be secured with lines and the bow allowed to swing round with the wind. This even works for singled-handed sailors, as the example shows. The skipper just has to haul the bow line in and afterwards doesn't need to be concerned with mooring lines.

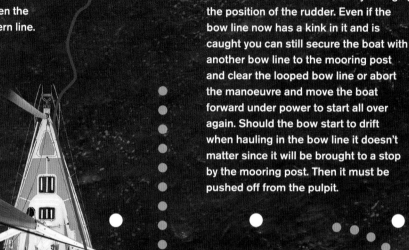

3 When the bow is free and the stern has swung round in the right direction you can use a gentle burst ahead on the motor with the rudder hard over in the direction of the turn to bring the boat to a stop. The burst on the motor will make the stern swing round, while at the same time the wind will blow the bow round. If the turn goes far enough you can leave the lane forwards.

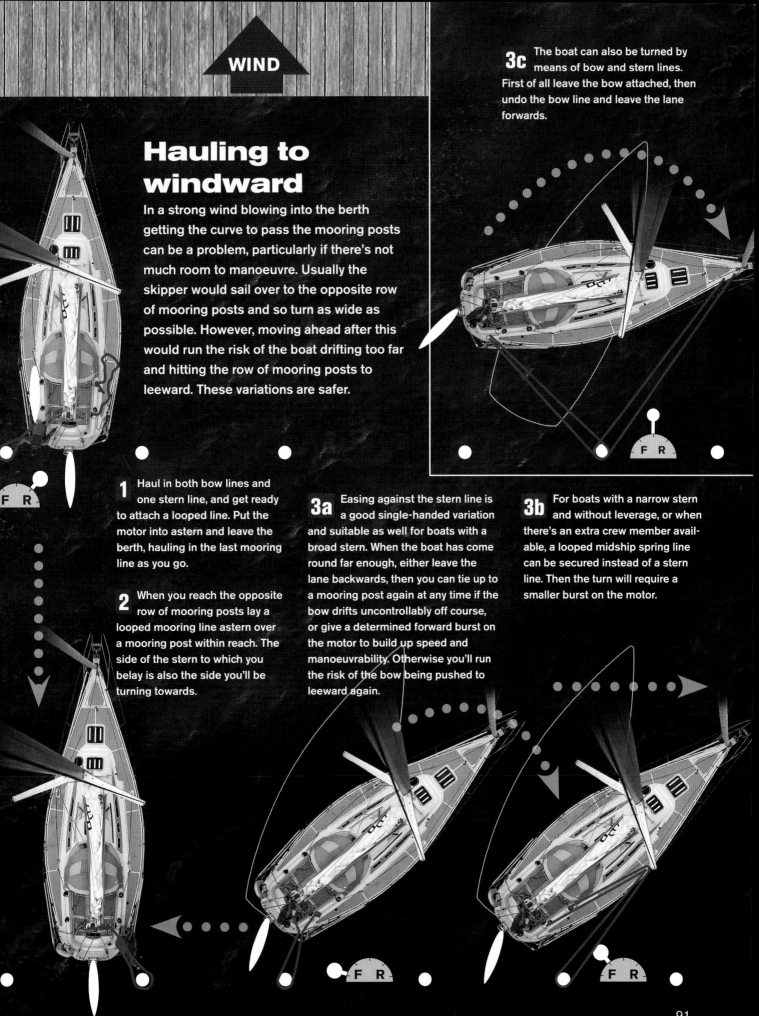

WIND

Hauling to windward

In a strong wind blowing into the berth getting the curve to pass the mooring posts can be a problem, particularly if there's not much room to manoeuvre. Usually the skipper would sail over to the opposite row of mooring posts and so turn as wide as possible. However, moving ahead after this would run the risk of the boat drifting too far and hitting the row of mooring posts to leeward. These variations are safer.

3c The boat can also be turned by means of bow and stern lines. First of all leave the bow attached, then undo the bow line and leave the lane forwards.

1 Haul in both bow lines and one stern line, and get ready to attach a looped line. Put the motor into astern and leave the berth, hauling in the last mooring line as you go.

2 When you reach the opposite row of mooring posts lay a looped mooring line astern over a mooring post within reach. The side of the stern to which you belay is also the side you'll be turning towards.

3a Easing against the stern line is a good single-handed variation and suitable as well for boats with a broad stern. When the boat has come round far enough, either leave the lane backwards, then you can tie up to a mooring post again at any time if the bow drifts uncontrollably off course, or give a determined forward burst on the motor to build up speed and manoeuvrability. Otherwise you'll run the risk of the bow being pushed to leeward again.

3b For boats with a narrow stern and without leverage, or when there's an extra crew member available, a looped midship spring line can be secured instead of a stern line. Then the turn will require a smaller burst on the motor.

WIND

1 To sail away single-handed run a long, looped bow line to windward and take it back into the cockpit. Otherwise a crew member can take this bow line over the foredeck. If you can find a helper on land, or even better on the next boat to windward, the line doesn't have to be secured with a loop knot. Undo both the old bow lines and pull the boat out of the berth by means of the stern line. Haul in the leeward stern line, set up the windward stern line with a loop knot and walk forwards with it on the boat. That way the hull of the boat will be held on the windward side. If there's just one person on board this doesn't apply. Meanwhile the bow line is paid out steadily.

2a It's now quite safe to let the boat turn to leeward, particularly in a very narrow lane. However, you can only achieve this with someone on a neighbouring boat helping or with another crew member. When the bow is level with the row of mooring posts, stop briefly and attach a bow line to the mooring post to windward. Push off the bow, if necessary. As soon as the boat has swung round you can sail forwards out of the lane. A single-handed sailor can help himself by using the leeward mooring post as a turning point. But that only works if the pulpit doesn't jut out.

With a bow line

In a strong crosswind a boat without bow thrusters can only be manoeuvred out of a berth under control with the help of lines. It's important to sail away from the leeward mooring post since this is the one the boat is being pushed against. Three variations are given here for sailing away, depending on the direction of prop walk, the number of crew aboard and the width of the berth lane.

2c If the lane is big enough you can also sail as far as the row of mooring posts opposite. A fairly strong forward burst on the motor with the rudder hard over should bring the boat on course. In a very strong wind and with the boat's bows being blown downwind there is however a risk of reaching the other row of mooring posts before the turn has been completed. Then method **2a** could be used instead.

2b Leaving the lane stern first is only advisable if prop walk is helping or at the very least not working against the turn. A clockwise propeller would move the stern here to port when sailing stern-first, but the bow would be blown in the same direction and hinder the turn. One solution would be as shown on the right-hand page. On the other hand, if the boat were to come out of one of the lower berths, prop walk would move the stern to windward or stop it on the spot while the bow moved to leeward, thus assisting the turn.

A running bow line with remote release: a line with two eyes is fastened to the worry line and belayed to the cleat. The eye in front is joined to a line which reaches to the cockpit.

2 By easing out slowly against the looped aft spring line the boat is hauled out of the berth and at the same time the stern is kept from drifting off course. As soon as the bow is between the mooring posts undo the bow line, either by remote control or a crew member can take care of it. The bow now swings to leeward, the stern to windward.

1 Haul in all mooring lines except the windward stern line. The bow is prevented from drifting by a running bow line (see photo). When the windward mooring post is within reach fasten a looped aft spring line to it.

With a worry line and an aft spring line

This variation shows how the stern can be held to windward by means of an aft spring line when the boat is to go backwards out of the lane and then forwards with the wind (so to the left). Here in addition a worry line is attached forward from the windward mooring post to the jetty. So it's also very suitable as a manoeuvre for a single-handed sailor. There's no long bow line, so it's not necessary to ask someone else to help.

3 Once the bow has swung round far enough the aft spring line is hauled in. You can now motor on through the lane either forwards or backwards. The aft spring line is also the correct aid if you have to manage without a crosswind, so in a very narrow lane or turning angle.

With wind power

It doesn't get any easier than when the wind does the work. This is suitable for all types of boat and wind directions between ahead and offshore broad reach. Fenders must be lowered at the stern. If it's wide enough then instead of pushing off you can also ease against the stern line which then acts as a spring line.

WIND

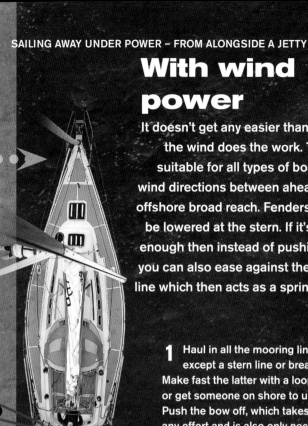

1 Haul in all the mooring lines except a stern line or breast line. Make fast the latter with a looped line or get someone on shore to undo it. Push the bow off, which takes hardly any effort and is also only necessary when the wind direction is from ahead.

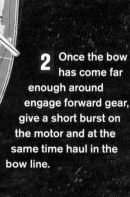

2 Once the bow has come far enough around engage forward gear, give a short burst on the motor and at the same time haul in the bow line.

Easing against the aft spring line

This is suitable for all wind directions between parallel with the pier and onshore. But this method is only recommended for boats with a broad stern, since they need a leverage effect. It's also recommended for single-handed sailors.

WIND

1 Attach a looped aft spring line (or a helper throws it to shore), and make sure there are plenty of fenders between the stern and the pier. Engage reverse gear and give increasingly strong bursts on the motor. The rudder angle doesn't make any difference, since when the motor is going backwards the blade isn't affected by the current and has no effect.

2 The bow swings round due to the leverage effect. When it's gone far enough give a short burst forwards on the motor with the rudder amidships so that the stern doesn't knock against the pier. If the boat is clear aft lay the rudder hard over away from the pier to turn the bow against the wind.

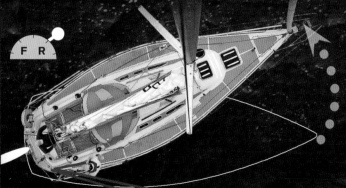

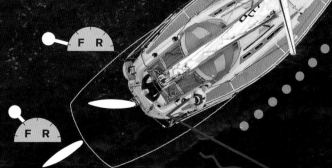

Easing against the stern line

This manoeuvre is only suitable for boats with a broad stern, but for boats like this it's quite brilliant. Wind direction: onshore to parallel. Only the stern needs to be fendered, and the motor remains in forward gear, so the sometimes anxious moment of changing course doesn't happen. It's very suitable for single-handed sailors.

1 Attach a looped stern line from the water side. Rudder hard over to landward, a powerful burst forward on the motor. The water hitting the rudder blade pushes the stern away, the leverage effect makes the bow swing round.

2 As soon as the stern is free of the pier slowly turn the rudder to amidships and if necessary, depending on the strength of the wind, reduce the thrust. Haul in the stern line.

Easing against the forward spring line

WIND

This is the only method for older, narrower boats to push away from a pier in an onshore wind without a bow thruster or the help of someone else. The bow must be well fendered since a great deal of pressure is concentrated in that area.

At a certain angle, depending on the shape of the bow, it's no longer a good idea to use the fenders like this. So engage reverse gear quickly and give a powerful/strong burst astern on the motor so that the boat doesn't drift back to the pier. Give the command, agreed on beforehand, to cast off the bow line and haul it in. If the person on shore doesn't move fast enough the manoeuvre won't be successful. On the other hand, a looped bow line always runs the risk of getting caught. The skipper must weigh this up carefully.

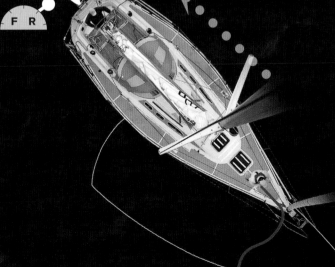

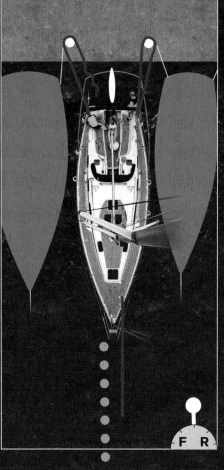

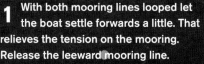

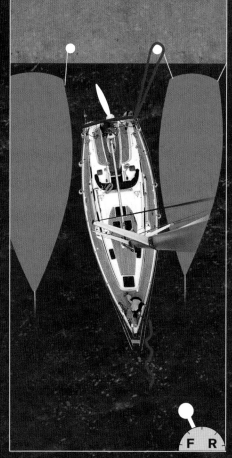

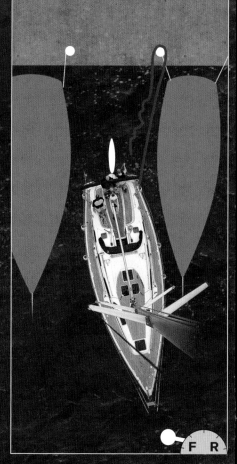

1 With both mooring lines looped let the boat settle forwards a little. That relieves the tension on the mooring. Release the leeward mooring line.

2 The helmsman eases gently against the windward mooring line with the rudder in the opposite direction, the bow-man casts off the line from the mooring.

3 Once the line from the mooring has sunk, give a strong burst ahead on the motor and haul in the windward mooring line.

Standard sailing away manoeuvre

WIN

Sailing away from a pier is often more difficult than sailing away from a berth with mooring posts, because mooring posts hold the boat away from neighbouring boats for as long as is necessary in a crosswind and are also reliable fixed points for spring lines. Therefore when berthing at and sailing away from moorings or an anchor it's also normal to drift towards the neighbouring boats. No-one takes offence at that. At least, not as long as the boat's sides are well fendered and the crew are also there to fend them off. But please only fend off on the toe-rail or the side of the neighbouring boat or on its pulpit or stern pulpit or its shrouds – never on the supports or wires of its railings; these can be torn off the deck.

It's very important when sailing away that the helmsman waits until the bowman gives the signal that the line from the mooring has sunk down far enough before giving a burst ahead on the motor. For if it gets caught in the propeller there will be chaos. And another tip: don't forget the third mooring line (the power cable)!

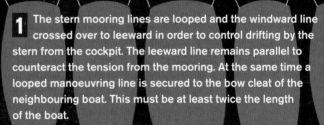

1 The stern mooring lines are looped and the windward line crossed over to leeward in order to control drifting by the stern from the cockpit. The leeward line remains parallel to counteract the tension from the mooring. At the same time a looped manoeuvring line is secured to the bow cleat of the neighbouring boat. This must be at least twice the length of the boat.

Cast off the leeward stern line first. That way the mooring pulls the boat away from the pier a little and the stern swings gently to windward. Now release the line from the mooring, which is easier to do now that the tension on it has reduced. Once this is free, give just a short burst ahead with the motor to push off the stern. By doing this the windward stern line which crosses over to leeward is paid out in a controlled manner. At the same time the bowman pays out the forward spring line. A few metres later the angle of the stern line becomes too acute and can't stop the stern from drifting off course any longer. Haul in the line and fender the stern against the neighbouring boats. This can also be assisted by gently turning the rudder, which moves the stern to windward. Nevertheless, the boat must still be fendered there.

WIND

Turning with a forward spring line

In a narrow Mediterranean marina the lanes are often narrower and at the same time the boats tied up there are long. Leaving the berth in the usual way isn't possible in that situation. Before the stern could get free the bow would ram the boat tied up opposite. Even turning with a bow thruster can be a problem if there's a strongish crosswind blowing because sometimes the impeller can't compete. In this situation the use of a forward spring line is an option. That way the boat turns directly round the bow of the neighbouring boat. Of course you should ask her skipper first, so that he's on board. Usually he also helps, so the manoeuvring line doesn't have to be attached with a loop knot. He can even cast it off. In this case it's a relief that the lines from the mooring rise up so steeply in the water and that there's no danger of them getting caught on underwater obstacles or the propeller.

2 The turning of the boat is now controlled simply by paying out the forward spring line and with gentle bursts on the motor. Look out for the bow of the neighbouring boat, lower fenders and keep out of the way! The anchor often sticks out and easily causes scratches and injuries, and can also easily get caught in your own railings. If the bow is pointing in the right direction the forward spring line can be released and pulled through. The helmsman takes over control with the rudder and the motor.

WIND

1 Secure a spring line over the neighbouring boat to windward, haul in the leeward mooring line and release the line(s) from the mooring. Give a burst astern on the motor and slowly pay out the windward mooring line. Pay out the spring line. If the angle with the windward mooring line is too acute to be effective any more, haul this line in too. Push the bow, which can now shift quite hard to leeward, towards the neighbouring boat and keep it well fendered. Turning the rudder has scarcely any effect here.

F R

2 Particular attention must now be paid to the line from the mooring belonging to the neighbouring boat on the windward side since the boat is moving forward with the rudder. So it makes sense to move a little further out of the space before the spring line is made fast and you begin to make the turn with it. Once the stern has come far enough around give an extra burst on the motor to pick up speed and haul in the spring line at the same time.

F R

Turning with an aft spring line

Sailing away backwards in a strong crosswind is not quite so much of a problem as sailing away bow first, since the bow drifts off course more than the stern (weathervane effect) and assists the turn to windward. But an aft spring line can be used to give better control. However, it's much less effective than a forward spring line since the leverage between the drive and the fixed point is noticeably less favourable. The sequence is practically the same as the example on the previous page.

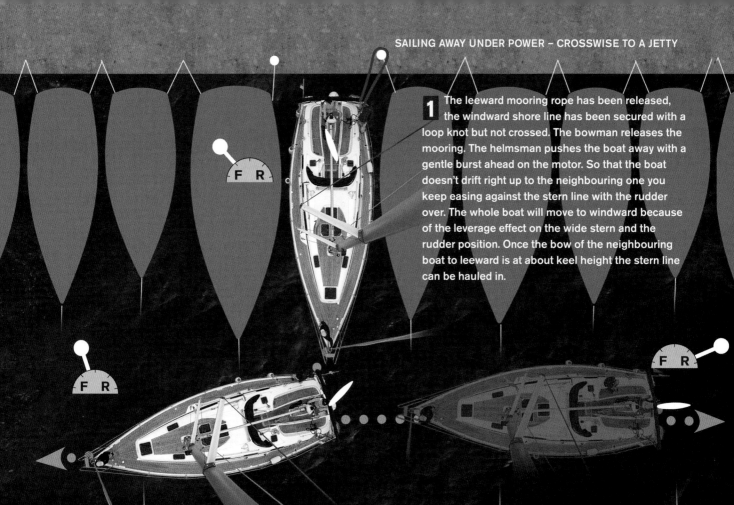

1 The leeward mooring rope has been released, the windward shore line has been secured with a loop knot but not crossed. The bowman releases the mooring. The helmsman pushes the boat away with a gentle burst ahead on the motor. So that the boat doesn't drift right up to the neighbouring one you keep easing against the stern line with the rudder over. The whole boat will move to windward because of the leverage effect on the wide stern and the rudder position. Once the bow of the neighbouring boat to leeward is at about keel height the stern line can be hauled in.

2 Now the boat is moving resolutely to leeward – so make sure it's well-fendered and fended off the other boats and look out for the neighbouring boat's mooring. The wind does the real work by pushing the foredeck in a curve to leeward.

3 Once the boat has turned round completely pick up speed with a strong burst on the motor to compensate for the momentary loss of manoeuvrability.

Backwards and across

This variation is suitable when no forward spring line can be attached to the neighbouring boat since it doesn't require the owner to be there (though this is rarely the case), or when other circumstances, such as a railing net, make it impossible. The design of the boat can also make it impossible to turn her bow, as there may be bow fittings which stick out a long way or even a protruding gennnaker boom or jib. This method can also help when the lane is so narrow that there just isn't enough space to turn. It has another advantage over sailing ahead: because of the weathervane effect of modern boats, the boat straightens up by itself and the lane can be cleared more easily than by sailing ahead.

However, this manoeuvre is only suitable for sailing away if the moorings fall away very steeply.

Otherwise the keel would get caught in the mooring of the neighbouring boat to leeward.

1 In an onshore wind both stern lines may be released together. It makes it easier if some chain has previously been inserted. In an offshore or crosswind, however, the looped line should remain attached, with a crosswind it should be the windward line. This is now paid out slowly and controls the sideways drifting of the stern. Haul in the anchor chain as well. In a strong offshore wind you can also increase control with a short burst astern on the motor.

2 The bowman indicates the direction of the anchor to the helmsman by means of hand signals. This is particularly important in a crosswind when the approach is curved rather than a straight line. If the bow isn't pointing to the anchor increase the load on the chain. The bowman also warns if the boat is approaching faster than the anchoring gear can be hauled in so that she doesn't sail over it.

3 The anchor must be up and down just before you reach it so that it can be broken out by the residual speed of the boat when you sail over it. If it's very muddy the anchor can be held just under the waterline and left there until the current has washed it clean. But you shouldn't sail too fast when doing this. Finally haul the anchor right up and secure.

WIN

Hauling in the anchor

In actual fact sailing away with the help of the anchor is easy. This is because the foredeck, which is particularly susceptible to a crosswind, is secured by the anchoring gear against drifting off course. However, there is one reservation as to why tying up with a Mediterranean moor is not always the most pleasant way. That's when the anchor absolutely refuses to come up because it has either become caught for some reason or because the chain of someone else's anchoring gear is lying on top of your own. In the first case only breaking out hard will help or if all else fails a diver, unless it can be broken out with a tripping line, as shown on page 123. An anchor buoy would be even better, but in harbour they get in the way. The second case, when one chain crosses over the other, can be remedied by the method shown on this page. Apart from these two small possible hiccups, sailing away with the help of the anchoring gear is actually one of the easiest harbour manoeuvres. However, if you're chartering a boat there is one thing you should be careful of: boats these days are usually fitted with electric winches and long chains or hawsers. This leads to the boat being pulled to the anchor by the chain over the winch. However, doing that can easily overload the winch. Therefore always let the motor finish off your own work and only use the winch to haul in the slack in the chain.

Freeing the anchor

In a crowded harbour your own anchor often gets caught on someone else's chain. If this is very heavy or tightly stretched your own anchor remains entangled in it no matter how often it's hauled up and paid out. A tripping line can be connected to the anchor chain to fix this. It should be at least the depth of the water plus the freeboard in length. With the help of this line the anchor can then be folded up under water so that the other chain slips off it. If one isn't available the method shown will help.

1 Pull the anchor up until the other chain is within reach. In an emergency dive down to it for Step 2.

2 Pull a strong line or a mooring line in a loop round the chain and push it through, with a winch if necessary.

3 Lower your own anchor. It can slip out of the other chain since this is fixed. Then it will come free.

Off the hook

It's worth your while practising sailing away under sail – because in addition to being good seamanship it's often the only option.

In the days when motors weren't necessarily fitted on sailing boats and were anything but reliable there used to be no question whether you had be proficient in sailing away under sail. It was simply necessary in order to leave harbour. By contrast, modern technology makes sailing from a standstill an almost forgotten art. Motors are long lasting and reliable, and harbours are often too narrow to be able to manoeuvre in safely. Which is why not using a motor is forbidden in a number of places.

And yet the manoeuvre should be mastered. Why does every beginner learn that when sailing away the sails should be ready to set even though they will be leaving harbour under power? Because the auxiliary drive can always break down and the safest motor for a boat is simply the sails. Many not so rare scenarios lead us down this path, such as motor defects and the motor service

facility only available in the next harbour. Only those who have mastered their boat without a motor can manage.

However, you shouldn't always and under all circumstances sail away under sail. Especially in high season the harbours are usually crowded and there's very little room to manoeuvre so that the motor should be used instead for reasons of safety. This is true in particular for those who are chartering boats, who don't know how their boat handles well enough as is necessary for risk free manoeuvring.

However, this should be practised when there is no possible threat of danger. In light to moderate conditions, for example in the outer harbour, in a fishing port with plenty of room or in your home marina when there's not much activity, in the low season for example.

Basic rules

An anchorage, not a starting grid
Safety must be paramount when planning manoeuvres. The most important question is: is there enough room to leeward? If there isn't the boat must be moved to a suitable place, for example out of a narrow mooring lane to its end.

Turning the rudder only when moving
A boat must pick up speed as quickly as possible, so that, especially in a modern short keeler, lift is created and drifting off course is stopped and so that at the same time the boat reacts to the rudder. Again, this is only possible if there's enough room to leeward.

Basic preparations
At the very least lay out one long manoeuvring line which doesn't have a tendency to kink. Also get ready all available fenders. Secure the mainsail with only a few gaskets ready to be set quickly. Discuss the planned manoeuvre in detail with the crew in a relaxed atmosphere and consider alternatives in case the procedure goes wrong.

1 To control the bow better and to gain time between the mooring posts attach a long bow line by means of a loop. Haul in all the other bow lines and pull the boat with the stern between the mooring posts. In addition use a stern line (here to starboard) as 'propulsion' for a crew member to pull the boat astern. At the same time pay out the bow line. It's difficult to do this alone, but there's no rush. The other stern line is looped over as an aft spring line. For a two-man crew the job of the man in red can be taken over by the helmsman.

Control to leeward

In an offshore wind the temptation to set the sails while still at the berth is great. In principle this works, however there is always the danger – and this increases as the wind increases – that the boat will drift across because of a gust or a careless manoeuvre. In addition the main boom or a sheet can get caught on a mooring post. Chaos reigns. It's simpler to set the sails once you've left the berth.

2 Pull the boat right out of the berth and loop the former starboard stern line now as a bow line. Now the sails can be set in peace. Clear everything away and check that the sheets are free to run. Keep the headsail, if set, or the mainsail on the opposite side to the one on which you're leaving the lane, in this case to port.

3 As soon as the turning manoeuvre begins and the bow has passed the mooring post in the right direction, haul in the bow line. The boat now turns, let the sails flap for the time being. The turning point is the starting point for the aft spring line, this prevents the stern from drifting to leeward. As soon as the bow has come round far enough haul in the aft spring line and at the same time set the sails and pick up speed. Tip: the aft spring line should only be operated on boats which have a strong tendency to drift without speed, such as short-keelers, because if it can't be hauled in smoothly or gets caught then the whole manoeuvre ends in disaster.

WIND

2 The mooring line is attached on the windward side, that is to the jetty or another boat. It's no use if the person there tries to haul in the boat, the risk of losing the line is greater than the benefit. As soon as the mooring line is belayed on board all other lines can be taken in. The crew now hauls the boat to windward hand over hand or with a winch. As soon as the other row of mooring posts is within reach loop a mooring line over a post astern.

Against the wind

If the wind is blowing into the berth just sailing away without the help of a tow is impossible. But if this isn't available you have to find a way round it to leave the berth. One way, if a little laborious, would be to move the boat out of the berth and along the mooring posts to the end of the lane, the whole time on a lee shore. That's not really practical. It's easier if a fixed point to windward is available. This could be an anchor taken out by a dinghy, if there's enough room available to windward. Or the row of mooring posts or the pier could be used. In addition a line can be taken there by the dinghy or, if that's not available, introduced from the windward side, as in this example.

1 A line is brought from a boat in the mooring lane opposite or from the jetty. This can be done by means of a fender which is moved by the wind. However, the line must be light and buoyant so it's best to use a pilot line. The heavy mooring line is held by the pilot line. If the mooring line and the fender come from your own boat there's no equipment to be given back at the end.

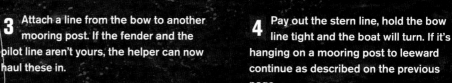

3 Attach a line from the bow to another mooring post. If the fender and the pilot line aren't yours, the helper can now haul these in.

4 Pay out the stern line, hold the bow line tight and the boat will turn. If it's hanging on a mooring post to leeward continue as described on the previous page.

With the wind abeam

This manoeuvre works in every case when the angle of incidence of the wind is up to 90 degrees. The more the wind blows from an offshore direction, the easier it is; the further it deviates in direction over 90 degrees onshore, the more difficult it is (until it becomes impossible). Finally it becomes a lee shore, in which the sails can hardly be set and from which you can hardly free yourself, as with a fixed point to windward (see left).

1 It's important when leaving the berth to keep the windward line under tension and thus in particular to stop the bow from drifting off course. This can be done by means of worry lines (as on the left) or with a long bow line looped over or operated by helpers.

2 Hauling out of the berth should follow quickly, or there's a danger that the stern will drift round too early and get stuck between the mooring posts. The wind will take over the turn itself.

3 For a clearer description the boat has been moved over to leeward a little here. Usually the windward mooring post of the berth can be used to tie up the boat with a bow line. As soon as the boat is lying with the bow into the wind the sails can be set. Finally release the bow line, hold the headsail aback and turn the bow so far that you're at least on an upwind course. Trim the sails and pick up speed. Of course this only works if the next line of mooring posts to leeward isn't close by. If it is you must move the boat to the end of the lane before you set the sails.

WIND

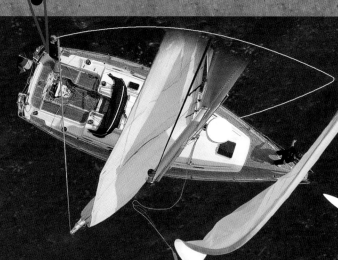

1 Set the genoa; if the wind is coming a little more ahead than abeam also set the mainsail. Release the lines. Usually the bow swings faster to leeward than the stern. Fender the stern. Slowly haul the sails in close. However, if other boats are lying ahead at the jetty a stern line should be looped over. Then the boat can't pick up speed ahead uncontrollably.

With the wind

It's very easy in an offshore direction, you simply let yourself drift away from the pier. Usually the bow drifts faster so that the boat automatically sets off on course. If it drifts ahead or astern more than abeam up to parallel with the pier a stern line should be used especially if space is tight.

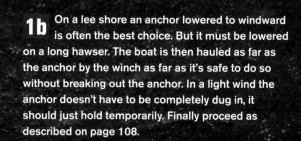

1b On a lee shore an anchor lowered to windward is often the best choice. But it must be lowered on a long hawser. The boat is then hauled as far as the anchor by the winch as far as it's safe to do so without breaking out the anchor. In a light wind the anchor doesn't have to be completely dug in, it should just hold temporarily. Finally proceed as described on page 108.

1a An after spring line takes over the 'propulsion'. A bow line isn't suitable since this would pull the bow towards the jetty. It's a good idea to get someone on shore to cast off, then the spring line doesn't have to be attached with a loop knot. It can be taken in either by hand, when the crew is large enough, or over a winch. If you can find enough people to help on shore you should take the spring line and go along the pier with it, at the same time getting up as much speed as possible.

Against the wind

This is the most difficult sailing away manoeuvre under sail. In an onshore wind getting away without someone else to help is practically impossible. This manoeuvre can only be attempted as pictured in a light wind or a small light boat. In addition a great deal of space at the pier will be needed. Therefore you should basically consider first of all whether the crew can haul the boat to a more suitable starting point.

The purpose of this manoeuvre is to accelerate the boat through tension on the after spring line as fast as possible so that it becomes manoeuvrable and can move away from the pier. It must also be protected with all available fenders on the leeward side. The manoeuvre begins below left on the opposite page. An alternative would be to lower an anchor.

2b If the wind is coming more ahead than abeam you must delay setting the sails until the boat has turned. Too early and the drifting of the boat would only put it back on the pier. After the turn it must be done quickly because the boat usually loses speed. This is where it becomes clear why this manoeuvre should only be attempted in very moderate conditions.

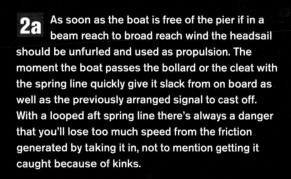

2a As soon as the boat is free of the pier if in a beam reach to broad reach wind the headsail should be unfurled and used as propulsion. The moment the boat passes the bollard or the cleat with the spring line quickly give it slack from on board as well as the previously arranged signal to cast off. With a looped aft spring line there's always a danger that you'll lose too much speed from the friction generated by taking it in, not to mention getting it caught because of kinks.

With the anchor

A big advantage of the Mediterranean moor is that when sailing away the anchor provides a fixed point to windward. This makes it possible to sail away under sail whatever the wind direction.

2 Stop hauling in the hawser just before you get to the anchor and wait for a moment until the boat has oriented itself to the wind direction. Then set the sails.

3 As soon as the sails are set haul the anchor up and down and break out. Fall away, pick up speed and leave the harbour.

1 This is easiest in an onshore wind. Simply take in the stern lines and haul the boat to the anchor. A mooring line astern from the lee quarter should be looped over a bollard to windward in a crosswind, to hold the stern to windward for as long as possible. Fender well to leeward. In an offshore wind the stern should be controlled by a looped stern line until it's clear of the other boats and so avoid sideswiping them.

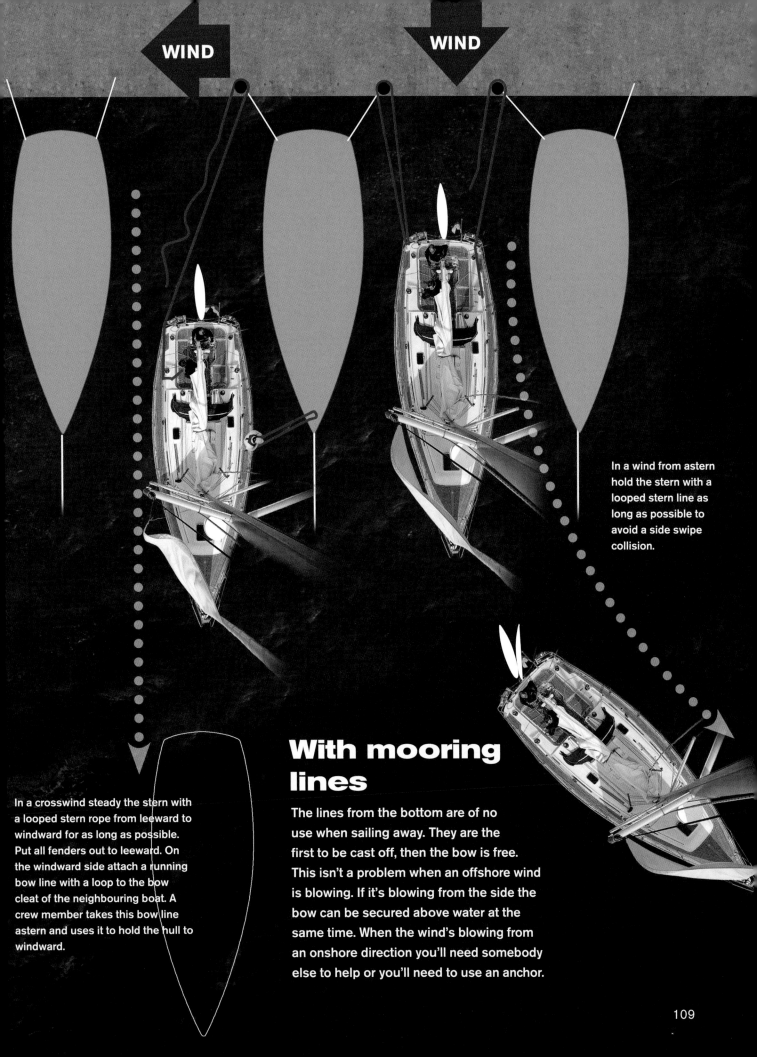

WIND

WIND

In a wind from astern hold the stern with a looped stern line as long as possible to avoid a side swipe collision.

With mooring lines

The lines from the bottom are of no use when sailing away. They are the first to be cast off, then the bow is free. This isn't a problem when an offshore wind is blowing. If it's blowing from the side the bow can be secured above water at the same time. When the wind's blowing from an onshore direction you'll need somebody else to help or you'll need to use an anchor.

In a crosswind steady the stern with a looped stern rope from leeward to windward for as long as possible. Put all fenders out to leeward. On the windward side attach a running bow line with a loop to the bow cleat of the neighbouring boat. A crew member takes this bow line astern and uses it to hold the hull to windward.

WIND

Nothing new, just narrower

The fact that in many harbour facilities many sterns stick out unprotected into the lane is a negative that becomes noticeable in particular when sailing away under sail. The motto 'first haul away, then sail away' is even more important here. But since sometimes there's no other alternative than to leave a berth under sail here are some variations of the examples already described. They work, but they assume a good knowledge of the responsiveness of the boat.

Nothing works against the wind without a fixed point to windward. Here a manoeuvring line attached to a fender is sent out from the windward side, so the boat can be turned towards the windward jetty.

The sails, hanging to leeward, are easily set. When sailing away an aft spring line with a loop could help to prevent drifting off course (see page 103).

110

1 With the wind abeam it's difficult
in harbour facilities like these to
cushion a turn because there aren't any
mooring posts, instead the other sterns
are the mooring posts. Therefore you
have to work even more than usual with
lines and fenders. The boat is hauled by a
forward spring line which has been run
out to the neighbouring boat and back to
the helmsman. An aft spring line secures
the stern against drifting off course.

2 In spite of all the lines to leeward the
boat is pushed against the finger
pier, therefore fender it well on that side
and fend off.

3 As soon as the boat is lying into
the wind the sails can be set.
Lower as many fenders as possible to
protect against the neighbouring boat
as well as the finger pier. Let go the
bow lines, set the headsail aback to
fall away. A looped aft spring line
stops the stern from drifting onto the
next boat to leeward.

Anchor manoeuvres

Cramped conditions and noise in harbour – but it doesn't have to be like that. Sailors find what they're looking for in secluded bays: peace and quiet in an idyllic setting.

The most wonderful thing about anchoring is the moment just after the motor has been switched off. Tranquillity – this one word stands for much of what sailing should really be all about. Solitude, relaxation and natural environment are associated with tranquillity. All the more astonishing then that relatively few sailors are searching for this tranquillity. That they would rather take part in afternoon rallies for the best berths in the harbour just to lie cockpit to cockpit, and share the smells, noise and activity of the neighbouring boat only a few metres away.

How different it is lying at anchor. The gentle splashing of the waves on the hull, animal noises on land, dozing in the cockpit scantily clad or even wearing nothing at all, bathing off the side of the boat, an unimpaired view of the sunset – you only get that Robinson Crusoe feeling lying at anchor. And then the next morning: absolute quiet over the water, perhaps a couple of wisps of mist. And on top of that the special satisfaction that comes from successfully completing your duties responsibly. Or to put it another way: having that good feeling that you're lying securely and you've done everything right.

This chapter should help you to get that feeling. And it should take away the fear that the anchor won't hold, which is the most frequent argument used against anchoring. Anyone who can overcome this fear can open up a whole new world of experiences. And also, sailing trips with overnight stays at anchor can be planned in a completely different way from when you only sail from harbour to harbour. So new horizons are open to you.

In the end handling anchors and chains is just good seamanship. This is because for various reasons, such as fog, currents, storms or an equipment failure on board, anchoring may be the only way to avoid danger to both crew and boat.

Therefore the various anchor manoeuvres should be not only a part of good training, but also every skipper should himself get more training through regular hands-on practice, if only during the midday siesta-time.

Equipment and preparation

With the right equipment and a few helpful tricks the manoeuvres aren't just safer, they are also simpler and more precise. What every skipper should check out before setting out.

1 The strain should be taken off the chain after the manoeuvre to spare the winch and to avoid clicking on the bow fittings. A knotted or shackled line can be used, but you can also get special chain claws. **2** Shackle secured with cable ties to avoid unintentional opening. **3** One buoy for every anchor on board. They don't just mark where the anchor lies, their line can also help when breaking out. **4** Don't secure the end of the chain with a shackle to a metal eye in the anchor locker. It can sometimes be necessary to let the chain run out, a shackle may then be under too much tension or already corroded. It's a

better idea to lash the end of the chain. **5** Then you know it can quickly be cut loose. The chain should have length markers at regular intervals so you can check how much has already been paid out. **6** There are special plastic clips for this, or variously coloured cable ties or lashings can be used as colour codes on individual links. A hawser can be marked with a waterproof pen or whipping. You can lengthen chains with special connecting links, however the breaking load will be reduced. **7** A spare anchor and anchoring gear should also be part of your equipment. Anchoring gear with a mixed cable is

ideal, lines made of lead that are often used make little sense. They hardly save you any weight and are also liable to damage from obstacles on the bottom. The next best thing after a mixed cable, webbing on a reel on the stern is very suitable. **8** So that the anchor can turn into the right position on the bottom it should be connected to the mixed cable by a swivel, all the more so when only chain is inserted. Otherwise the anchor can screw in by spinning; if tension is then placed on it torque on the anchor results. **9** An anchor weight can reduce the swinging circle in a light wind or help the anchor to dig in at a flat angle.

More space in narrow bays

When a bay is already very full there is really only one reasonable rule of conduct: head for another bay! However, reasons such as an emergency on board or a gathering storm can leave no other alternative but to still look for a space. The basic rule of thumb is that the swinging circle of another boat is forbidden territory. Modern boats especially swing considerably at anchor, they literally sail to and fro, because the surface area pressure point over the waterline lies a long way away from the centre of lateral resistance. There are ways of reducing the swinging circle, as well as further tips and tricks for as many crews as possible to benefit from a sheltered bay. One very important rule should however be followed by everyone when doing this: the more crowded the bay, the more important it is to have uninterrupted anchor watches and to be ready to manoeuvre.

Anchor-V

This method not only increases the holding power, it also decreases the swinging circle considerably as shown. It's also true that the bigger the angle the smaller the circle. The boat no longer moves to and fro but now just turns a little on the spot both ways. The disadvantage in a narrow bay is that in the event of having to make a quick getaway, such as when other boats begin to drift, it's more time-consuming dealing with two sets of anchor gear.

Anchor pack

This formation is the preferred choice of flotillas and is also a great space-saving solution for a short stop-over. For a longer stay, such as overnight however, boats should be moved apart since they're vulnerable to swell and can't react quickly to changes in the weather. Important: moor the boats with their rigs set so they don't collide in swell.

Riding weights

A heavy object which is lowered on the chain down to the bottom in order to decrease the swinging circle when there's little wind or current. Because of its resistance on the bottom the boat turns around it as though round an anchor. The spare anchor can also be used as a weight, however it's no longer available then for any other manoeuvre. This method is above all for your own benefit, since the boat lies more quietly. In a freshening wind the weight is pulled up because of the tension in the anchoring gear, and the swinging circle increases.

114

Stern line

A line made fast to shore can make another anchoring space available, because it stops the boat swinging. However, this method is only recommended for emergencies or a short stop-over since there is a danger of a lee shore if the wind changes direction.

Mooring buoy

Specially positioned mooring buoys limit the space conditions enormously. But usually you have no idea how much weight there really is below or how corroded the anchoring gear is already. Indications, not to mention guarantees, of the holding power are rare. When a buoy is already in position, in particular with a very large boat, you can in an emergency ask whether you may tie up there too (you can also do this for very large boats at anchor).

Ball and light

Anchor below, ball above – every sailor should memorise this rule of thumb, because the ball is required by the regulations for preventing collisions (COLREGS). At night it must be replaced by an anchor light, or it can be left in place as well. Both signals should be fixed in a position that can be seen from all sides. These signals should also be set out when shore lines have been made fast so that everybody knows that there is a vessel here that can't move out of the way immediately.

Stern anchor

A very effective method of preventing swinging. When it's narrow it's often a good idea to anchor normally to begin with and then to lower a second anchor using the dinghy.

Shore lines

Safe just like in harbour. The boat is made fast on all sides and is usually also well protected from winds by the shore. Therefore if the anchor should slip at all, you can ease against the stern lines with the motor.

Standard manoeuvre

A good anchoring manoeuvre starts in harbour. Is the necessary equipment on board (see page 113), how long is the chain, is there a rope, a second anchor, an anchor winch? If the equipment is right, then if you're inexperienced in dropping anchor or a charterer, and so can't possibly know about the characteristics of a particular anchoring gear, you really shouldn't choose the smallest and most crowded bay for your first attempt at anchoring. Not just to avoid any collisions, but also to avoid comments from the other skippers. A sandy bottom is ideal for a first attempt. All anchors hold best in this. On the other hand, holding power in mud is very much less, whatever the design of the anchor, on a stony bottom it's also more or less a matter of luck whether the anchor catches on something, and seaweed is the worst of all. Therefore when planning a sailing trip pick out all the most suitable places to anchor on your route. When you're doing this look out for all the possible obstacles, such as cables or wrecks. Places on the charts marked 'pollution' or 'ammunition' are no-go areas. The strategic location of the anchoring place is important – if the wind changes direction are you at risk of a lee shore?

1

Sail round the planned anchoring place at least once. The radius should be the same as that for the anchoring gear to be used. In this way you can discover any possible shallows or polluted sites as well as the nature of the bottom, and the skipper can be sure that there will still be enough water under the keel if the wind changes direction.

Rope or chain?

Which holds better, chain or rope? Outdated theories and stubborn prejudices often lead to uncertainty and incorrect buying decisions. Both materials have their defects and advantages.

A combination of chain and rope is best for holding an anchor. That way the strength of both systems is combined and their weaknesses mitigated as far as is possible. A chain is resistant to mechanical damage from stones or coral, its weight ensures a favourable angle of attack for the anchor when digging in, in addition it doesn't bring as much mud with it as a rope when it comes up and it runs through an anchor winch from beginning to end. Moreover, in a light wind it gives a smaller swinging circle since the chain sits on the bottom and the boat turns on a short vertical length of it. Therefore charter boats often use chain exclusively.

However, it increases the overall weight of the boat in the sensitive bow area and, more importantly, causes peak loads, as when jerked about by the swell, not absorbed by the anchor which can then break out. The assumption that the sagging of the chain works like a shock absorber has been disproved. The chain can be stretched taut, depending on the type of boat, by a wind speed of as little as 20 knots. Therefore it's better to use only ten metres or so of chain with rope for the rest of the length as necessary. This should allow as much stretch as possible to bounce the peak load, as it were.

WIND

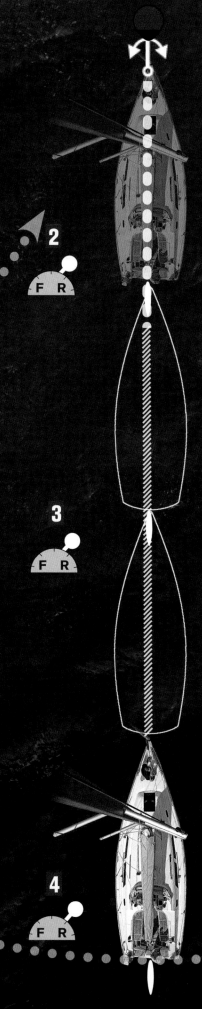

2 The helmsman turns the boat into the wind at the chosen anchorage. At his signal, when the speed ahead is more or less nothing, the bowman pays out the anchor in a controlled manner until it reaches the bottom. Except in harbour or in very deep water the position of the anchor should be indicated with a buoy. The wind pressure will now move the boat to leeward, in a light wind the helmsman gives a short burst astern. The bowman pays out at the same speed as the boat is moving so that the anchoring gear is lowered straight and the tension doesn't come on the anchor too soon nor does the chain or rope lie in a heap.

3 How much chain or rope? It's important to add the freeboard to the bow to the depth of the water, both of them together give the depth. If you're only anchoring for a short time such as a lunch break and the crew remains on board it may well be enough to use three times the depth for the anchoring gear. But modern anchors only develop their maximum holding power at an angle of less than eight degrees. However, this results in a ratio of 7:1 between the length of the anchor cable and the depth. In two metres of water and with a freeboard of one metre at least 21 metres should be lowered.

4 Once the right amount of chain or rope has been paid out you can begin to dig in the anchor. To do this, first go slowly astern a little so that the anchor has an opportunity to turn into the right position and the anchor cable isn't under too much tension. Give the anchor a couple of minutes to dig in deeply. With the help of a bearing on the shore or in the case of clear water by observing marks on the bottom, the helmsman knows when the anchor holds. Another good method is to put one hand on the chain/rope. Jerky movements mean that the anchor is rattling over the bottom. If you have to stay overnight or in rough weather, gradually increase the tension a little, depending on the engine system fitted. If the anchor breaks out too soon the anchor cable must be lengthened or a second anchor dropped. Incidentally, it's not a good idea to jerk at the anchor cable by going astern.

WIND

Dropping a second anchor

To increase the holding power of the anchor gear or to restrict the boat's room for movement, its swinging circle, it can be a good idea to drop a second anchor. It should be the right specification for the size of the boat and ideally equipped with both chain and rope, like the main anchor.

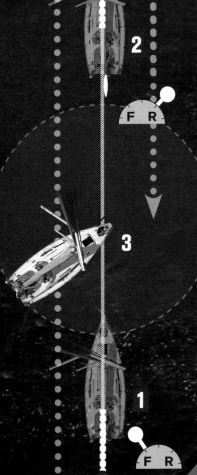

Bahamas style

1 This is suitable for anchoring in tidal areas or when the wind direction is changeable. First drop an anchor on a very long rope over the stern against the wind and/or current.

2 Then drop a second anchor over the bow. You can also start with Step 2, the order in which this is done doesn't make any difference. If the second anchor is dropped using a dinghy the rope for the first one doesn't have to be so long.

3 The boat swings around on its own axis if both anchors are belayed to the bow. On the other hand it remains stationary if one rope is belayed to the bow and the other to the stern.

Crossways and single-handed

1 An elegant manoeuvre which requires minimal effort and can be done single-handed. The boat is steered across the wind and the first anchor is dropped from the stern to windward. It can also be dropped from the bow, but this runs the risk of the rope fouling the propeller.

2 Once the correct length of rope for the depth of the water has been run out, it's belayed and the first anchor is dug in a little. Many boats now use the motor and rudder angle to balance out so that they remain lying diagonally to the wind. The helmsman can now drop the second anchor into the water from the bow when he's ready.

3 The second rope is now paid out as far as the first, then belayed. If the first rope has been fixed to the stern, first belay the slack line to the bow, then unfasten it from the stern so that the boat turns with its stern to leeward (see also pages 56–7). Dig in both anchors.

CURRENT

Loading the dinghy

A First the rope comes into the boat, in neat bights, so that kinks can be avoided later. **B** Then put the anchor on top. **C** Secure the anchor to the dinghy. **D** Attach a pilot line to the end of the anchor rope. Now the anchor can be rowed out. The pilot line is particularly important when rowing out so that you're not working against the weight of the heavy rope. Drop the anchor, then use the pilot line to haul in the dinghy with the man and the rope as it runs out. Haul the rope on board and secure.

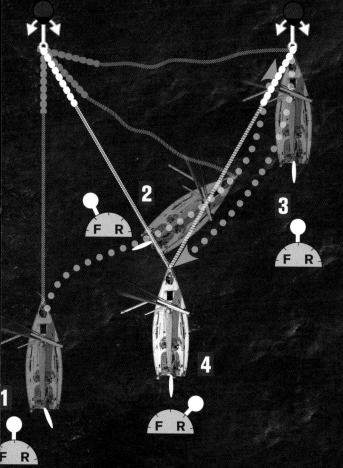

Under power

1 The boat lies correctly at anchor. Whenever the wind freshens or the swinging circle needs to be reduced (see also page 114) the second anchor can be taken to its place with the help of the motor.

2 Motor a little way in the direction of the tension on the first anchor, then turn and steer diagonally to windward until the first anchor is lying crosswise. There should be no or very little tension on the anchor rope, otherwise the first anchor may break out.

3 Once the second anchor has been dropped the wind will move the boat to leeward. You need to pay out the same amount of rope as for the first anchor.

4 When both ropes are attached, dig in the anchor by slowly moving astern.

With the dinghy

1 The initial situation is the same as for setting the anchor under power. However, this way others lying at anchor will be less troubled by engine noise and also there's less risk of the first anchor breaking out. The disadvantage is that the transverse distance between the anchors can only be estimated.

2 The anchor plus mixed cable and/or rope is placed in the dinghy. The end of the rope is joined to a worry line which is paid out with it from on board.

3 The second anchor is dropped and marked, the rope and the worry line are hauled in until both anchor ropes are the same length.

4 This way you don't have to row against the drag of the anchor rope which, depending on its weight, can be impossible. Dig in both anchors again.

Four specific anchoring methods

Information on charts about stony bottoms, rapidly decreasing water depths and extensive shallows isn't necessarily a reason for abandoning plans to anchor. Otherwise parts of the skerries and large areas of Turkey, for example, would be virtually unknown to sailors. Certain specific techniques allow you to anchor confidently where there are no shallow, sandy bays available. However, since you can quickly be faced with a lee shore when the weather changes, an anchor watch should be assigned or at the very least an anchor alarm set up, either through GPS or depth sounder. There is another specific anchor manoeuvre for single-handed sailors. Anyone who sees this carried out perfectly will not be able to suppress a little nautical jealousy.

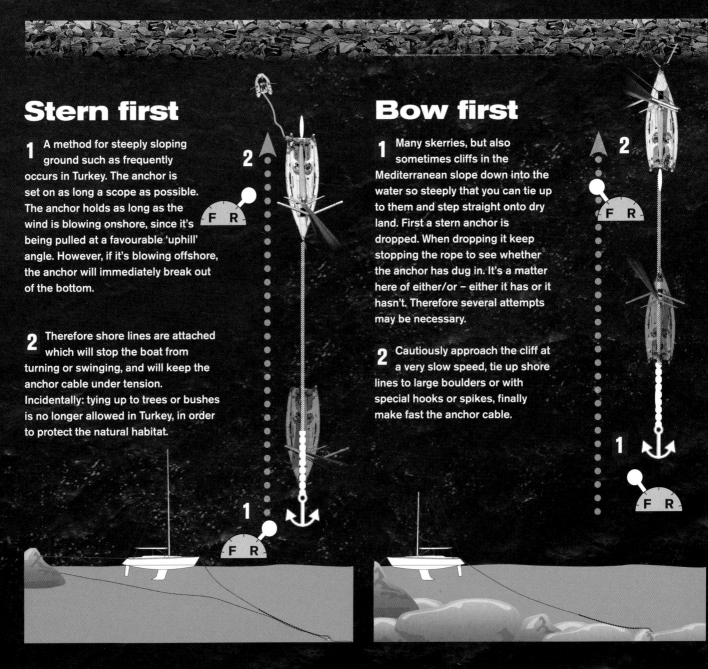

Stern first

1 A method for steeply sloping ground such as frequently occurs in Turkey. The anchor is set on as long a scope as possible. The anchor holds as long as the wind is blowing onshore, since it's being pulled at a favourable 'uphill' angle. However, if it's blowing offshore, the anchor will immediately break out of the bottom.

2 Therefore shore lines are attached which will stop the boat from turning or swinging, and will keep the anchor cable under tension. Incidentally: tying up to trees or bushes is no longer allowed in Turkey, in order to protect the natural habitat.

Bow first

1 Many skerries, but also sometimes cliffs in the Mediterranean slope down into the water so steeply that you can tie up to them and step straight onto dry land. First a stern anchor is dropped. When dropping it keep stopping the rope to see whether the anchor has dug in. It's a matter here of either/or – either it has or it hasn't. Therefore several attempts may be necessary.

2 Cautiously approach the cliff at a very slow speed, tie up shore lines to large boulders or with special hooks or spikes, finally make fast the anchor cable.

Shallow water

1 Sometimes a long, shallow beach falls away sharply to a great depth. Not an ideal place to anchor. But if you still want to stay there, even just for a swim, you'll need two anchors. The first is dropped where the water is deep and holds well since it's being pulled 'uphill' by an onshore wind.

2 The stern anchor can be dropped from the boat or from a dinghy and stops the first anchor from breaking out in a sudden offshore wind. If the second anchor is dropped far into the shallows it sometimes has to be dug out by hand.

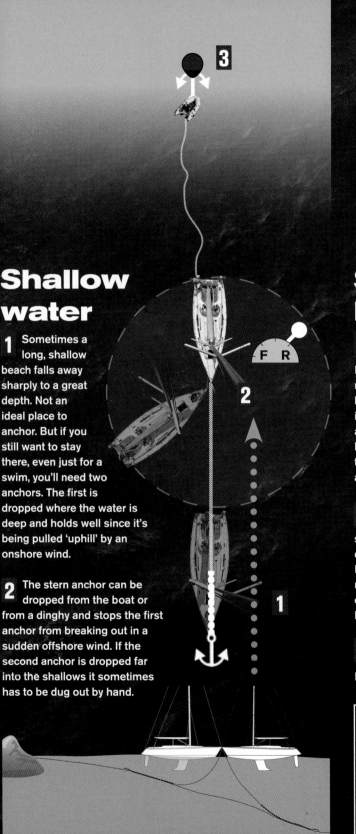

Single-handed

1 An elegant swing that no-one but a single-handed sailor should master. It doesn't work with just a chain. The mixed cable should be stowed in a bucket at the stern. The end of the rope is attached to the bow (diagram below) and taken outboard via the stern. The helmsman lets the anchor drop from the stern and pays out the mixed cable and the rope.

2 If the anchoring gear is long enough, he belays the rope to the stern and waits until the anchor has dug in by means of the wind pressure. He can help things along with the motor and that way has very good control over the boat since the rudder has the current streaming over it.

3 The rope at the stern is unfastened, the stern swings around and the boat now has its bow into the wind.

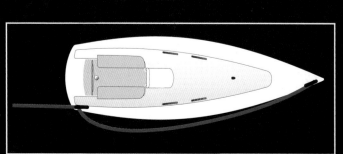

Under sail

Dropping the anchor at an anchorage and hauling it back in without the aid of a motor is also a fine art – and here especially very useful too. Because you can try it out at your leisure in bays. Somebody who arrives late or weighs anchor early won't be short of friends if they can do this without making a noise.

WIND

Standard

1 Approach the anchoring place with the headsail handed or rolled away. That creates space on the foredeck. Sail head-to-wind (see page 62/63).

2 As soon as the boat has stopped drop the anchor then pay out the rope in a controlled manner, depending on the drift speed.

3 Once the required length has been paid out make fast the rope, let the sails flap for a little while or set them back so that the anchor digs in. Then take them in.

Single-handed

1 The approach takes place before the wind with a minimum of sail. Drop the stern anchor at the chosen anchorage.

2 Once enough rope has been paid out make it fast and sail into the anchor with sail power.

3 Belay the rope to the bow and the boat swings round (see also page 121).

Breaking out

Usually the anchor line (and with it the boat) is hauled in by hand until it's up and down. When the anchor comes away from the bottom sail away and pick up speed.

1 If the anchor doesn't come away let out plenty of line again to make an approach under sail. Sail up as close to the anchor with as much speed as possible, taking in the slack on the line.

2 Just before the boat sails over the anchor make the line fast. The weight of the boat should now free the anchor.

Weighing anchor

Getting the anchor back on board is basically the standard anchoring manoeuvre in reverse. That is, first the helmsman sails slowly in the direction of the anchor. The slack from the rope is taken in by hand, or over an electric winch. It's important when doing this that the boat isn't pulled towards the anchor either by a hand or electric winch or even by hand. That can overstrain both the mechanical system and the crew members. The work is done by the propeller. One person on the forecastle should indicate the direction to the helmsman so that he doesn't put tension on the chain or the rope with a course that's on the diagonal. Stop the motor just before the anchor and take the anchor up and down as far as is possible. Usually you now only have to wait for a moment before the anchor comes free of the bottom. Should it have got caught preparations such as in the box below will help. But you can also give the rope or chain a bit more slack. The boat then slips astern a little and the helmsman can now try to break out the anchor by swinging round. Be careful, scratches on the hull from the chain are almost inevitable. Another method is to load the foredeck with as many people as possible, take the anchor up and down and then order everybody astern. The leverage effect will put a great deal of tension on the rope.

Avoid stress with a tripping line

When the anchor absolutely refuses to come out of the bottom only a diver can help – unless the anchor gear was carefully prepared.

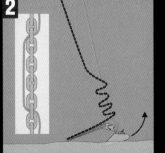

A tripping line has a very simple function: it's attached to the head of an anchor and pulled in the opposite direction to that in which the anchor has dug in. This helps when the anchor is wedged fast under a rock or some other obstacle, or has caught on another chain. It can be attached in several ways. **1** For instance, in combination with an anchor buoy. Doing this as illustrated has the advantage that the buoy reacts to fluctuations in the water level but doesn't exert any pull on the anchor which could lead to it accidentally breaking out. If the anchor is set firmly the tripping line is always accessible via the buoy. **2** If a buoy can't be used – as in harbour (since it could foul the propeller of another boat) – then attaching the tripping line to the anchor chain and bringing them up together is another possibility. It can be threaded through every fifth link or so. If the tripping line is then pulled tight and the chain released, it slips down the line and the anchor flips round. **3** It also works to tie or shackle the line, which should be a little longer than the depth of the water, to a link which will be found above the water line when the chain is pulled taut.

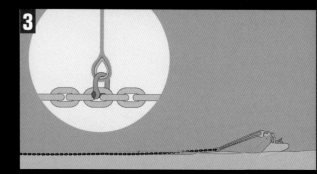

A member of the DGzRS (*Deutsche Gesellschaft zur Rettung Schiffbrüchiger*, German Lifeboat Institution) throws across a tow line.

KODEN

⊗VEGESACK⊗

Towing

Securing the towing line correctly

If you need to be towed you should know how to deal with the rope and how two boats are linked together. This chapter describes important tips and tricks for securing the towing line correctly.

Lifeboatmen are required to take on a tow for various reasons. Older diesel or inadequately maintained motors often break down. But not even the most conscientious owner is immune from breaking down and needing a tow from someone, be it in a dead calm or after running aground, not to mention worse things. Likewise anyone can quickly find themselves in a situation where they can offer a tow, as the spirit of good seamanship obviously demands, so long as the person towing doesn't thereby endanger themselves. So it's a good idea to master the basic rules.

In this chapter the most important aspects of towing are summarised. In this regard the skipper must bear this in mind as a matter of principle: towing is generally a dangerous undertaking, but particularly so in rough conditions. A rope that breaks or fittings that are torn out can injure someone, therefore only those who are absolutely necessary should be on deck. No-one should be in a potential danger zone, as for example the pulpit. Hand signals should be agreed between the skippers, at the very least for slowing down and stopping – the most common will be described.

Preparations for tying ropes together

As a general rule the lifeboatman throws over his own rope which already has a yoke with two eyes spliced into it. These just need to be attached to the two forward cleats and the towing can begin. This approach has several advantages: the rope is designed for the job and isn't just any old rope. The simple fixing doesn't demand too much from a stressed or panicky crew.

However, this method places all the tension on just the cleats, which can lead to them being pulled out in a swell or by a powerful jerk. But on the other hand the rope under tension can't work itself free. Another possibility for securing the line is with a loop around the mast when this is keel stepped. In doing so the loop must be secured against riding up. The method

described has proved itself to be particularly suitable since it distributes the tensile load over many points. The main load is taken up by the winches which are designed for strong pulling. The tow rope loop should be prepared already before the arrival of the lifeboat, then its rope just has to be secured. If a long tow is likely the rope should be secured as shown.

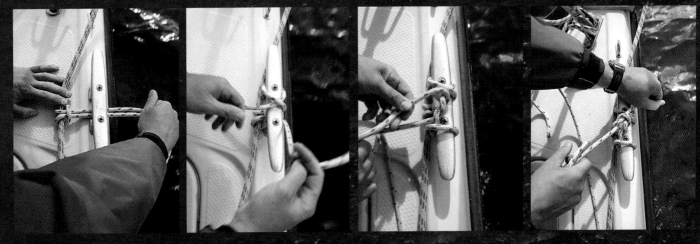

Tie a loop in the middle of a strong line and take both halves through and over the cleat. If there are no spring cleats available use the genoa sheet leads. Lash the line round with short lines, and if a long tow is likely, protect against chafing, for example with cloths. Attach to the winches.

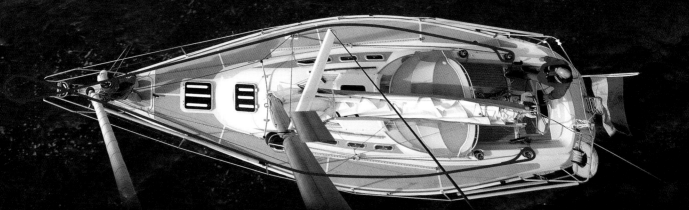

As long a rope as possible

The tow rope should be as long as possible, the optimum being five times the length of the boat. In addition it should have a good deal of stretch in it, to cushion the jerks. The cushioning effect increases with the length. In high seas the length should be adjusted so that both boats are in the same part of the wave system. The towing speed must be adjusted to the boat being towed. If this can't achieve planing speed it can be towed at its theoretical hull speed.

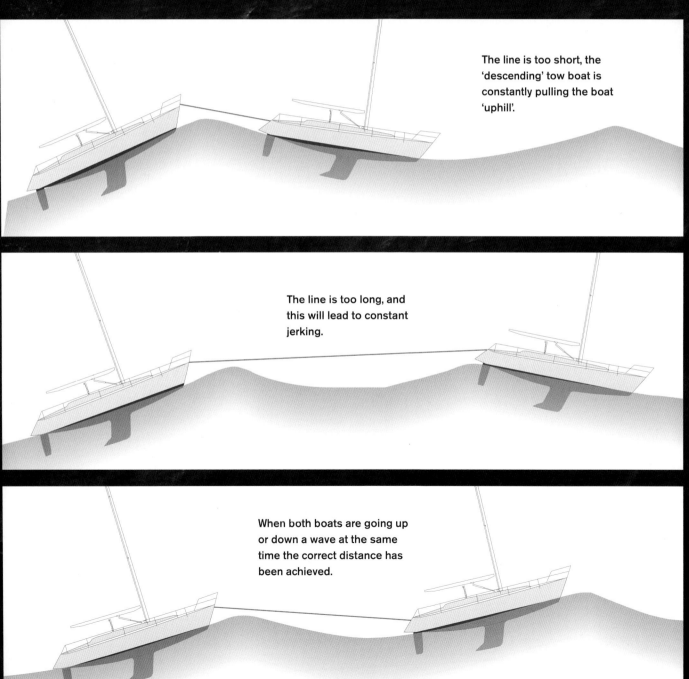

The line is too short, the 'descending' tow boat is constantly pulling the boat 'uphill'.

The line is too long, and this will lead to constant jerking.

When both boats are going up or down a wave at the same time the correct distance has been achieved.

4 The tow boat continually sails ahead on the diagonal to avoid hard jerks. Carry the rope along until it becomes taut, then leave the foredeck.

Tying up to the towboat

In a non-emergency situation, as in a dead calm or when the motor has failed, procedure should be agreed with the towboat. If you're dealing with a professional you should follow his advice as a rule.

3 Attach the rope under the guardrails and free of obstacles in the direction of the tow, either to the cleats or by means of a pre-prepared yoke.

1 The lifeboat approaches to within throwing distance. To avoid any problems the foredeck should be clear of any lines, the sails should have been taken in and secured safely.

1

2 The line is thrown over. This can take several attempts, therefore keep absolutely calm and don't react by rushing about and screaming.

A yoke to the towboat

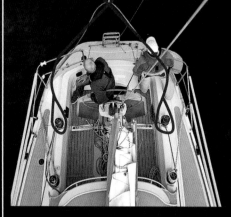

Also when your own boat is doing the towing the tensile load on the rope must be distributed over as many points as possible. To do this attach a strong line as a yoke round the stern onto the winches. The winch platforms must also be designed to take tension astern, which is usually the case with cruising yachts. The cleats only serve as guides, they also take care of friction when changing direction. After slowly starting to tow the yoke can thus be adjusted and in addition the rope can also be thrown off under load.

Communicating with hand signals

If normal communication over VHF is interrupted or if one of the parties doesn't have the equipment available, voice communication can be impossible due to wind or engine noise. Hand signals can provide clarity.

The thumbs up is the universally accepted signal for 'All OK!' or 'Well done!'.

Waving a line up and down on the foredeck means: I need a tow, please give me a tow.

Once the rope is made fast on board and everything is ready for a careful tow the arms are crossed in front of the body.

A circling motion with a raised arm means that the towboat can increase its speed.

Should the towboat need to reduce its speed outstretched arms in front of the body are moved up and down.

Jerky sideways movements of the elbows with bent arms signals the towboat to unfasten the rope.

Parallel towing: side by side

Parallel towing is a suitable method of providing very controlled aid for another boat, for example when trying to control a leak. The towboat can directly influence the boat being towed. Therefore you should change from towing with a rope to parallel towing when you're near or in the outer approaches of a harbour. The boat being towed can then be manoeuvred directly into a mooring space, instead of having to hope, once the rope has been cast off, that there's enough speed left to reach a berth. It's important to be well fendered between the boats when parallel towing. Because of the risk of damage this isn't suitable in high seas, particularly for two sailing boats where there is a risk of their rigs colliding.

1 The towboat approaches from astern and takes or hands over the first line, depending on whether he's located to leeward or windward. This line is attached to the towboat as a forward spring line.

2 The forward spring line on the towboat is attached to the stern of the stricken vessel. Tying up like this transfers the impetus of the towboat which can also take in the slack and get nearer in a controlled manner.

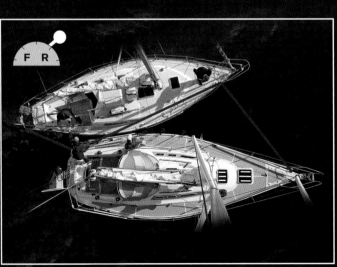

3 An after spring line from the towboat is attached which will take the strain when stopping. Finally a forward breast line is used to adjust the distance between the hulls.

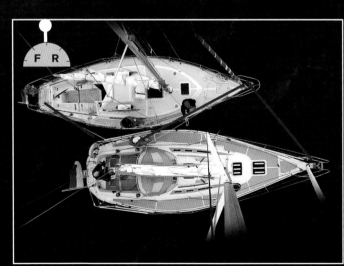

4 Fendering is very important. In addition, the stern of the towboat must project behind the stern of the boat being towed. This is the only way that allows the tug to steer whilst the two boats are tied together.

Man overboard

The most important thing in an emergency is to go back immediately for the person in the water. There's no standard manoeuvre for this, rather there are several variations. In this chapter the relative advantages and disadvantages are explained.

Sequence of steps

1. Mark the scene of the accident

Throw a lifebelt, a life-saving collar, a marker buoy or something similar to the person in the water. Press the MOB button. If possible detail a member of the crew to do nothing else but watch the person who's fallen overboard and to point to them with an outstretched arm at all times. Call for help on the VHF radio and a mobile phone but only if a crew member can be delegated to do this. For a two-man crew it's important that the person left on board doesn't lose visual contact.

2. Start the MOB manoeuvre

The immediate reaction, depending on the intended manoeuvre. Announce the planned manoeuvre loudly, maintain calm. Start the motor and begin supporting action while giving some attention to lines.

3. Recover the person

After a successful approach prepare rope connections and secure the person. Decide on which side and with which method they should be rescued. Often it's advisable to take in the sails first, but a boat hove to can also provide a stable platform. If the recovery is unsuccessful this is your last chance to call for help.

Woman overboard: the most important thing now is to go back for her as fast as possible.

Very few people die while sailing because they've fallen overboard. Up to now in Germany you can count the number of victims per year on the fingers of one hand. One reason for this gratifyingly low figure, which statistically makes sailing on the whole one of the safest hobbies, is simply that people rarely fall overboard, because in really rough and dangerous conditions only a few people venture out. These are mostly experts who know how to move around safely on their boats. Moreover, forecasts and warnings are so reliable that major surprises in the weather occur less and less frequently.

On the other hand it's much more probable that someone will fall overboard in moderate conditions, in sunshine and gentle seas. Miscalculation, lack of care and alcohol are the causes of an unintentional bath. The crew remaining on board should know what to do so that this doesn't end in tragedy. The greatest danger for the person in the water is that the boat will get too far away from them and that the crew will be unable to find them again. Even in calm conditions a couple of dozen metres is already enough, when, for example, it's late afternoon and the person is disappearing against the light.

Every skipper should be clear that there's no magic formula for a correct manoeuvre. There are many man overboard manoeuvres taught which are equally important/ relevant/necessary/good/effective. But as a rule modern boats are equipped with reliable and powerful motors and their short keels turn easily. In addition setting and taking in sails are much faster and smoother operations these days and of course can be done from the cockpit.

In these conditions one course of action in particular is called for: do an immediate quick stop, regardless of whether you're on a downwind or upwind course, and start the motor immediately. Whether you take in the sails first or go back to the person in the water with the sails still set or the sails remain tight or thrown off depends on the type of boat and the circumstances. In the same way a completely different manoeuvre can be successful, for example if there's no motor at all or only a low-powered outboard motor available. Precisely because the equipment is so different and sailing boats vary so much you should practise with your own boat once every season or once every holiday in a charter boat so that you know which manoeuvre is the right one. After all it should remain just a statistic.

WIND

2 The sails must be taken in as soon after as possible. If this means that the boat moves too far away from the person in the water it's better sometimes to make another approach with just the mainsail and then take the sails in again.

Approach under power

This is the manoeuvre of choice for boats with a reliable, powerful motor and furling sails or sails that are easy to hand. It's particularly suitable for small or inexperienced crews, particularly in heavy seas and strong winds with distractions such as flapping sails or uncontrolled drifting. If the sails have already been taken in the helmsman can concentrate completely on the approach course.

However, this manoeuvre carries a danger with it which shouldn't be underestimated: the crew can become so preoccupied with taking in the sails that they lose sight of the person in the water. Therefore going head-to-wind should take place immediately after the accident, and taking in the sails may be left until you're getting near to the person in the water. To avoid injury from the propeller the motor must be cut, whichever manoeuvre you choose, as soon as the person in the water is near the boat.

3 If the sails have been taken in make for the person in the water at full speed. Reduce speed in good time before you reach them.

1 Immediately after the accident luff into the wind, no matter whether you're on an upwind, beam reach or downwind course. Start the motor and engage forward gear. Start to take in the sails.

4b

Direct approach: the helmsman bears down on the person in the water and stops immediately next to them. To make it possible to stay near them as soon as possible, a line can be thrown to them. The boat lies with the stern into the wind and automatically aligns itself in the wind direction like a weathervane. You can steer backwards to the person in the water so that they're always in sight and can also be taken in over the stern. However, this variation is only recommended in moderate conditions. In heavy seas the stern going up and down can have the effect of a pile-driver and can kill the person in the water. Moreover, waves can also come over the stern.

4a

Indirect approach: should the boat lie with the bow into the wind when near to the person in the water, and in choppy seas, very windy conditions or in a cross current, you'll have to sail around in another half circle. Make this half-circle as tight as possible and as close to the person in the water as possible, so you don't lose sight of them.

Munich manoeuvre

This variation can also be carried out by just one person. The idea is to let yourself drift in a controlled manner into the immediate vicinity of the person who's gone overboard. That assumes a particularly fast reaction time. The manoeuvre should – more than any other – be practised with your own or a charter boat, since the direction and speed of drifting of every boat depends on its hull form and the design of the attachments and they are all different. Because of their smaller projecting lateral surface area short keelers drift strongly without propulsive speed ahead, unlike long keelers. Modern boats with fully battened mainsails or rigging with angled spreaders on which the main boom can't be let out as far as 90 degrees, often keep going ahead at quite a considerable residual speed when hove to. Since the direction of drift is hard to influence only when under sail the motor should definitely be used to help. A disadvantage of this manoeuvre is an occasional strongly flapping mainsail, which for inexperienced crews can be an additional stress factor.

2 During the turn the foresheet remains tight so that the jib or the genoa is held aback after the turn. Ease the mainsheet until the boom is against the shrouds. Start the motor.

3a When hove to the boat starts to drift, so try with backwards and forwards bursts on the motor to hold the direction towards the person in the water.

1 The turn should really follow as fast as possible so that you remain close to the person in the water. But if this doesn't work at first, an approach can take place later drifting with gentle bursts ahead on the motor and thus easily controlled. If the starting position is a beam reach the foresheet must be held taut before the turn.

3b If you can't hold the direction towards the person in the water you'll have to gybe or sail a Q-turn. Both manoeuvres are described on the following pages.

4 The manoeuvre can be finished off by turning and then heaving to, alternatively the sheets can also be let fly or the sails taken in.

135

WIND

1 Turn as soon as possible after the accident, with all sails remaining sheeted in. Bear away immediately. Be careful when doing this because the boat can briefly heel over sharply.

The sails sheeted in with this manoeuvre and the motor is used to help. That's why it's very suitable for the single-handed sailor and for inexperienced crews, since no sheets have to be used and you can keep the person in the water in sight without distraction. However, this is absolutely not to be done in difficult conditions and is also not recommended for beginners since the sails can flap hard and at times the boat can heel over sharply.

Turn, gybe, turn

2 The boat straightens up and the motor is started now at the very latest.

3 Pass as close to the person in the water as possible before the wind, that gives both sides confidence. If available, throw out more life-saving equipment or try to establish a connection with a line.

5 For the second circle a wide turn was deliberately selected. This way when gybing and turning there's no unnecessary mad rush and the boat keeps swinging enough for it to be manoeuvrable with just the sails. But that takes it further away from the person overboard. Yet, if you sail in a tight circle the boat stops after the turn and can only be positioned right by the person in the water under power, but then the boat actually ends up close by them. Here too the manoeuvrability of the boat has an impact on the right choice.

4 The gybe which is necessary now should be no problem with closely held sheets and a well-timed change in course. However, the subsequent luffing can again lead to the boat heeling over sharply.

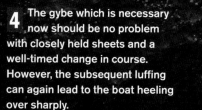

Only one turn

This manoeuvre, which is strictly called a Q-turn, can easily be executed single-handedly or by a small crew, as in the example opposite, since the set of the sails remains unaltered. Also, all the other advantages are the same, but there's one more decisive advantage: it only needs one turn. But this advantage is not without its compromise. For this manoeuvre to succeed the boat must first move a short distance away from the person in the water. A risk which should only be taken in good visibility and never in bad conditions! Incidentally, both manoeuvres can also be sailed without a motor but in that case the wind pressure is higher and at certain stages the boat heels, in addition it takes longer to reach the person in the water.

2 After the turn keep the sails sheeted in. While falling away the boat can briefly heel over sharply.

3 Sail downwind far enough for a gybe to be just avoided. That creates space for the next stage: going head-to-wind.

1 After the accident sail on for a few more boat lengths to make space for two complete circles. How far you have to sail depends on the manoeuvrability of the boat. Modern short keelers can turn almost on the spot, a full circle measures one to one and a half boat's lengths. With a boat like that four or five boat's lengths are enough. But for a ten-metre yacht that's a good 50 metres!

4 Position the boat by the person in the water by controlled sailing almost head-to-wind. By sailing almost head-to-wind the boat ends up lying on a high upwind course with its sails flapping.

137

Q-turn

This manoeuvre owes its name to the Q-shape of the course that is sailed. By doing a Q-turn on a beam reach or broad reach course you can dispense with gybing which can occasionally be a problem in stormy weather. It's still taught as a man overboard manoeuvre, but it's only suitable under very limited conditions. It was certainly the right course of action in the days when there were no motors, or only unreliable ones. Because the boat keeps on going and can be positioned exactly without having to depend on a motor. However, since not using the motor requires correct handling of the sails it's not recommended for inexperienced crews or the one remaining person on board, at least not in difficult conditions. Because of the effort involved in the operation on the

1 Fall off immediately on a broad reach and sail the troughs; that way the approach on a new bow side is easier. The motor can now be used to help, but the manoeuvre is described here without it.

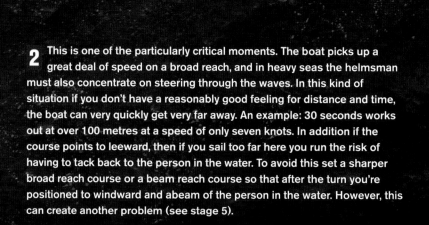

6 The Q-turn ends with a course nearly head-to-wind towards the person in the water. If a motor is available this is the last chance to start it, but it would be better to let it run during the whole of the manoeuvre.

2 This is one of the particularly critical moments. The boat picks up a great deal of speed on a broad reach, and in heavy seas the helmsman must also concentrate on steering through the waves. In this kind of situation if you don't have a reasonably good feeling for distance and time, the boat can very quickly get very far away. An example: 30 seconds works out at over 100 metres at a speed of only seven knots. In addition if the course points to leeward, then if you sail too far here you run the risk of having to tack back to the person in the water. To avoid this set a sharper broad reach course or a beam reach course so that after the turn you're positioned to windward and abeam of the person in the water. However, this can create another problem (see stage 5).

WIND

boat there are many distractions and delays which in the course of this manoeuvre can cause the boat to move a long way from the person in the water. So there's a great danger that you'll lose sight of them. You often find the term cow-turn, but this is not to be confused with the Q-turn. The cow-turn is carried out on a close-hauled course when a boat can't get its bow across the wind, like some classics. So the boat goes with the stern across the wind and luffs on the new tack onto a close-hauled course again. The term cow-turn comes from the behaviour of cows: they don't stand with their noses directly into the wind but turn, when they want to change sides, with their hindquarters across the wind.

5 After turning the boat should lie slightly to leeward abeam of the person in the water. This has the advantage that the speed can be easily controlled by lowering and close-hauling the sails. Were the course to lie noticeably further to leeward the sails would have to be furled. In modern rigging with angled spreaders, however, the main boom can no longer be eased off to 90 degrees, and the boat would therefore pick up speed again and you'd run the risk of missing the person in the water.

4 When turning only the genoa should be let fly. It can flap on the new tack, just the mainsail is all that's needed for a measured approach.

3 Once the turn has begun its size is determined by the diameter of the turning circle of the boat and the experience of the crew. The smaller the turning circle and the more precise the handling the sooner the turn can happen.

Gybing

A manoeuvre that brings the boat back to the person in the water very quickly. In moderate conditions the sails can remain sheeted in if there's a motor available (situation 1a); in which case gybing is suitable for small crews or a single-handed sailor. However, if the sails have to be used because there's no motor available or the conditions are stormy, then only really experienced sailors should attempt the gybe. Otherwise it won't work, chaos reigns and the boat quickly gets further and further away from the person who's fallen overboard.

WIND

1 The gybe under sail starts by slowly falling away. Sheet the sails in halfway.

1a Start the motor, give a full burst forwards, leave the sails sheeted in. The high speed will reduce the pressure in the sails.

2 After gybing, the genoa should normally not be kept sheeted in any longer, the mainsail is enough for propulsion, and the boat is more easily controlled this way.

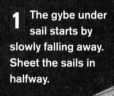

2a Stop just before you get to the person in the water and let the sheets fly.

3 Position the boat towards the person in the water by going almost head-to-wind.

140

3 As soon as you've established a connection you can decide which one to secure first: the person in the water or the sails.

Quick-stop

The quickest way to remain as close as possible to the person in the water when coming from a downwind course. It doesn't depend on the way the sails are set, so can be done under a spinnaker; however, the sails may be damaged by the violent beating.

2 Start the motor at the first opportunity and use it to help you.

1 Regardless of the sails, lay the rudder hard over to windward. The first priority is your closeness to the person in the water.

Which method for getting them back on board?

Wind

When the person in the water has been reached and a line established to them, the second, often more difficult, part of the rescue begins – actually getting them back on board. This is all the more of a problem if the person who's gone overboard can't help themselves. As a general rule of thumb getting someone back on board in heavy seas is more easily done on the leeward side than on the windward side, for the following reasons:

1 calmer water than to windward
2 boat moving towards the person
3 the side of the boat is lower because it's heeling over
4 using the wind to throw life-saving equipment

On the other hand, in moderate conditions

and when there is a swimming platform or a swimming ladder available bringing the person on board should take place over the stern. This offers the safest and lowest method of getting on board. However, it can be dangerous there in a strong wind if the stern is moving up and down in the swell.

There are various things that can help a person out of the water, such as the main sheet, a rescue sling, using the main boom as a crane or with a recovery cradle. Which of these actually helps depends mostly on the type of boat, the number of people on board and the conditions. Once again you should try these things out! If not with equipment that has been bought specially, then at least what you have on board, such as a main sheet.